Tales of Old

Stories from The Old Testament

Retold by Clive Johnson

Labyrinthe Press
www.labyrinthepublishers.com

Original content © by Clive Johnson.
First published February 2020.

All rights reserved. No part of this publication may be reproduced, distributed or transmitted in any form or by any means, without the prior written permission of the publisher.

Labyrinthe Press
Leigh-on-Sea, United Kingdom
www.labyrinthepublishers.com

Book Layout ©2013 BookDesignTemplates.com
Cover illustration ©2019 Universitaria
Distributed by IngramSpark and CreateSpace

British Library Cataloguing in Publication Data
Tales of Old/ Clive Johnson. —1st ed.
ISBN 978-1-9162276-2-0 (Print edition)
ISBN 978-1-9162276-3-7 (Electronic edition)
Also available as an Audible digital audiobook.

*Listen for what God says in everything you do,
and everywhere you go; he will lead you along
the right path.*

—PROVERBS 3:6 (interpretation)

*To Miranda, whose fascination with God's Creation
touches the hearts of all who know her.*

CONTENTS

Introduction 1

In the Beginning: The Story of Adam and Eve, and The Great Creation 7

The Story of Noah and his Ark 21

Abraham, The Man who was Faithful to God 33

Joseph and his Brothers 51

The Story of Moses and The Great Exodus 75

Joshua, God's Warrior.. 101

Samson, The Strong 119

The Story of Ruth, The Faithful 137

The Tale of David and Goliath, and David and Saul 149

Solomon, The Wise and The Wealthy 167

Elijah and The Evil King and Queen 181

Esther, The Brave 201

Job, A Troubled Man 215

Daniel, The Dreamer 229

Jonah, The Hesitant 251

Introduction

IN A 2019 Intelligence[2] debate, entitled *Old Testament vs. New Testament: Passion, Poetry and the World's Greatest Stories, Which of these two texts is the greater, in terms of message, literature and legacy?*,[1] the Old Testament won over the audience hands down. Its canon provides one of the richest works in English literature, not to mention the literature of many other tongues.

What sets this extensive collection of inspiring writings apart is its breadth. Its pages cover topics as diverse as the meaning of holiness to a vision for the end of times, as well as detailing the history of Israel, offering

---

[1] Old Testament vs New Testament: Passion, Poetry and the World's Greatest Stories, Which of these two texts is the greater, in terms of message, literature and legacy? Available at https://www.intelligencesquared.com/events/old-testament-vs-new-testament/, accessed 9 August 2019.

words of wisdom to live by, and laying down the law for an ancient people.

Its message of a forgiving God, but one who must be honored before all others, features strongly, while its many colorful characters have inspired writers, film makers, painters, composers and many more over the centuries.

Most of all, the Old Testament is a *book of stories*. These were written not just to be read–and at a time when very few were blessed with that particular faculty–but to be told to an enthralled audience, and preached by learned elders, in the true nature of the oral tradition. Following this great tradition, the stories in this book should ideally be read aloud.

Myths, elaborate illustrations, and actual factual accounts may all play their part. Yet here, the crucial purpose of the stories is not to entertain, but to inform, to urge to action, and often to warn. Each carries a powerful message that can be heard and understood.

Giants, fabulous creatures, and unworldly beings all feature. Celebrated leaders, maverick prophets, as well as good and bad kings and queens have important roles to play. Within its pages are described unfathomable miracles and celestial wonders, violent wars and the crushing of entire cities.

This collection of tales doesn't shy away from being candid, vivid, and even explicit in its descriptions.

We read about angels and demons, heroes and cowards, the lowly and the exalted. Exotic visitors from Arabia, kings with strange sounding names, and rags-to-riches princes all make their mark.

Many of the Old Testament's cast of characters live shadowy lives. Just a few remain faithful to God, and these are the individuals whose examples we are encouraged to follow.

The backdrop for much of the narrative is often dramatic–snow-capped mountains, sweeping deserts, whirlwinds, parting seas and a burning bush–all play their part. We even venture to the depths of the sea.

The selected collection in this book focuses on the better-known tales in the canon. Prescriptions of the law, psalms and proverbs, and the lives of many of the prophets are left for others to tell.

This retelling attempts to remain faithful to the message of scripture, if occasionally using artistic license, and not always relaying the full detail of what is contained in the books upon which it is based. Thus, for example, the dialogue between Job and his three friends is abbreviated, while the story of Noah is elaborated with fresh color.

These stories are written for children from around the age of five years and up, but should delight any reader. In writing and researching them, I have been touched by many of the messages, surprised to be shown something new in a story that I thought was very familiar to me.

This is the nature of scripture, of course–every reading brings something new, a lesson or purpose that's relevant for the moment. My hope and prayer is that this wonderful capacity for fresh interpretation isn't lost in this retelling.

So follow, as we now journey from a perfect garden into thorny wild lands, make an exodus from Egypt to a promised land, meet strongmen and scheming women, dive inside the belly of a giant fish, and watch an entire city crumble at the sound of a battle cry.

Let us huddle with Noah and his family inside his ark, marvel at the wisdom of Solomon, and feel Joseph's yearning for his father and family when he is reunited with his brothers.

These great stories of old have lessons aplenty to teach, and wonders to inspire. They are as fresh and meaningful today as they have always been.

Note: in keeping with common convention, honorific titles are used for God throughout this book. Pronouns referring to Him similarly use title case.

While aiming to remain faithful to scripture, an attempt has been made to introduce gender neutrality into the stories, as well as to feature the strong female role models that appear in the Old Testament, alongside the male. Thus, for example, Adam's gender is not stated until God creates Eve. The terms "person" and "human being" are preferred to "man", except where the latter is specifically intended within the context of the story.

Each chapter presents a different story, ordered in the sequence that these appear in scripture. Each is separately available as a short story on Kindle, and as an Audible audiobook.

CHAPTER ONE

In the Beginning: The Story of Adam and Eve, and The Great Creation

IN THE BEGINNING, there was only God. God's Word, what He wanted to happen, caused everything to be.

So it was, that our Earth, the Sun and Moon, and all the stars in the sky, were created by God. Before even all these existed, God still existed.

Then He created the Heavens and Earth, which was at first without its gently rounded shape that it has today. A great swirling mass of gases churned around in space–dark grey, growing and squeezing, not revealing what form it might take next.

God decided that out from the darkness, there should come light. And so, He commanded that darkness and light should be separated, making night and day.

And so it was, that the very first day came to be.

As the gases started to gather, and water appeared, God willed that they be separated into what we now see as the sky, and the waters that bob up and down as the sea. So, the blue sky and the blue seas became separated, making space for air to fill the void between them.

Morning came again, and then another evening–and so ended what we may call the second day.

On the third day, God decreed that the water of the seas be gathered together, making space for land.

When the land had formed, He desired that all sorts of plants and trees, grasses and ferns, and nuts and berries should come to grow upon it. Through their seeds, these would each continue to grow, providing food for the many animals and people that were later to be born.

Evening came again. And so ended the third day.

When morning came once more, God decided that there should be bright lights that should shine in the sky, both at nighttime, and by day. These would shine light, give guidance, mark out the times of the seasons, and the times for celebrating and remembering.

In the night sky, countless twinkling stars made their presence known. God set the Moon in motion, reflecting its light back to the Earth when nighttime came.

In the sky that appears each day, God made our glorious Sun to shine brightly, giving light so that everyone could see, and providing warmth to shield us from the bitter cold.

Evening came again, and so ended the fourth day.

God then saw that there should be creatures in the sea, and too, animals of many kinds that would fly through the air.

Through His Word, He caused sea creatures of all kinds to come to be, dwelling deeply in the oceans, and swimming freely in the rivers that rush down from tall mountaintops. Giant whales were created, and the tiniest angelfish. Sharks and swordfish, turtles and teaming trout–He gave life to them all, giving them His blessing so that they might multiply and continue to live through their offspring.

God gave life to all the birds of the sky, and to the butterflies and other flying insects too. He made powerful wings for the mighty albatross, so that it might be able to fly across an entire ocean. In different colors, and with so many different shapes and sizes, He created all the creatures of the air. Their squawks and heart-felt songs were like beautiful music to God's ears, and He loved them all, as He loves all of His Creation.

This, then, was the fifth day.

God saw His wonderful world, and all its living things, and He felt very happy with what had come to be.

On the sixth day, God decreed that there should be animals of many kinds to populate the Earth.

These too, He willed should multiply and give birth to others of their kind.

He made happen the coming of wild beasts, tiny field mice, and scurrying lizards. He allowed the giraffe to grow its tall neck, and the elephant its swinging trunk. Dogs and horses, lions and lemurs–these, and many other creatures of the land came to be, as God designed.

While his world was very beautiful, rich in variety, and constantly alive with color and movement, God felt that his Earth was missing a creature or a plant with whom He could have a special relationship. He desired that there might be one among His creation that had His own image, and who would be invested with intelligence and responsibility to care for His world.

So, God created humankind. To the firstborn of our own ancestors, He gave the name Adam.

God showed his new friend the wonderful world that He had created–a world filled with all kinds of sweet-smelling flowers and trees overflowing with luscious green leaves. He led Adam beside gently bobbing streams of water, to grassy meadows, and high mountain paths.

"I give you this place to rule over!" said God. "Take care of all My creatures that swim in the sea, and look after all the plants and trees, and the many animals that roam on the land!"

"Grow strong, and be happy. I give you My love and My blessing!

"For food, I give you all the plants that bear seed. For all the birds in the sky, and all creatures on the Earth, I give all the green plants, such that they also might eat.

"You are My beloved Creation! You are very precious in My sight, and it pleases Me to see that My Creation dwells together in harmony!"

After God had spoken, evening came again. And so ended the sixth day.

This is then the story of how our wonderful world came to be. When God had completed everything that He willed to be, He rested.

"This is my precious world," said God. "I am well pleased with it, and see that it is good!"

God decreed that the seventh day, the day that He rested, should be a holy day. So it is for us today, that we need not work every day, but should have time for rest. This is a day when we might especially remember everything that God has created for us.

When He created Adam, God breathed life into Adam's nostrils. As it was for Adam, every breath that we take gives us life, and connects us with everything that is.

God led Adam to a beautiful oasis that He had created. He called this "The Garden of Eden."

The garden was rich with many fine green plants and brilliantly blossoming flowers, for it was fed by the waters of four mighty rivers, which branched out from a single stream.

In the middle of the garden stood two giant trees–one that was known as the "Tree of Life," while the other was called "The Tree of Knowledge of Good and Evil."

The land was very fertile, producing rich fruit for Adam to eat. There was gold there, and shiny black onyx, and other precious stones.

The plants supported many kinds of life, which all lived happily together, for there was no reason for them to argue. God provided everything that they needed, and He commanded Adam to be their caretaker.

God gave Adam the fruit of every plant and tree to eat. But there was one tree that He warned must not be eaten from.

"You must never eat from The Tree of Knowledge of Good and Evil," warned God, "For if you take the fruit from there, you will surely die!"

Adam listened carefully to what God said, but did not understand His meaning.

Adam gave names to all of the creatures that God had created. One by one, God brought one of each kind before Adam. Some seemed more like His human creation than others–such as monkeys that could nearly stand on their hind legs, and parrots that could even speak the same words uttered by Adam!

God wanted Adam to have a special friend with whom he could share his life. Yet, none of the other animals seemed to be a suitable companion for him.

So God caused Adam to fall into a deep sleep. God then formed a second human being from Adam's own body. Adam he made male, and his partner, who later became known as Eve, he made female.

Adam said to Eve, "We are made of the same bones, and are from the same flesh. When we are together, we are as one flesh."

These first two people wore no clothes, but were not ashamed for being naked.

One day, while they were walking in the garden, Adam and Eve came upon a snake, who had coiled himself around the thick trunk of a tree, and slithered to the end of a strong, overhanging branch, from where he could raise his head to speak to the humans.

"The Tree of Knowledge of Good and Evil is here," said the snake. "Why do you not eat from it? Is it really so that God has told you that if you do so, you will surely die?"

"This is indeed what God has told us!" answered Eve. "We may eat from any other tree but this one."

"Oh, you foolish people!" teased the snake. "Do you really believe that eating the most delicious fruit that hangs from this tree will kill you?

"I tell you that you will not die! God knows that when you eat this fruit, your eyes will be opened, and you will see just as He does–knowing the difference between good and evil. This is knowledge that He does not want you to have!

"See, the fruit that hangs from the tree is waiting for you! See how ripe it is for picking!"

The snake continued to invite the curiosity of his human neighbors. Eventually, Eve was persuaded to try a small bite from the fruit of which he spoke, which appeared to be mouthwatering and too tempting to pass by. She offered a little to Adam, who also took a bite from the fruit that God had forbidden to be eaten.

In an instant, what the snake had claimed came to be true–the eyes of both Adam and Eve were opened to the existence of both good and evil, to what keeps them in company with God, and what separates them from Him.

Then they saw that they were naked, and they felt ashamed.

Quickly, they gathered thick leaves from the garden, which they sewed together to make simple clothes with which to cover themselves.

Afraid that God would be angry with them when He learned what they had done, they sought to hide. But God soon made His presence known, calling out to them, "Where are you hiding?"

The terrified couple came out to face God, knowing that they could not keep secret what they had done.

"We have eaten from the tree that You told us we must not approach," began Adam.

"Eve offered me some of the fruit, and this I took into my mouth."

"What is this you have done?" demanded God.

Eve then stepped forward to offer her confession.

"Mighty LORD, I am guilty for eating from this tree. I was deceived by the snake, who assured me that were I to eat from the tree, I would not die. Foolishly, I was led astray!"

God's heart was broken, because His children had disobeyed Him. From a place of such beauty and perfection, His human creation had sought out what they were not meant to have, and so separated themselves from always trusting Him.

"You are the most cursed among creatures!" God rebuked the snake. "From this moment forward, you will crawl upon your belly, ever close to being crushed under the foot of humankind! Yet too, you may strike at his heel, and there will be no friendship between you!"

"I will make you suffer pain!" God then told Eve in His anger. "When you give birth to your offspring you will suffer, and no more will you enjoy the many comforts that I have provided for you."

"As for you," God then addressed Adam, "You will roam the Earth in search of food and shelter. The rich abundance of fruits and fine green plants that grow in My garden will no longer be yours to eat for free. You will work hard, in fields that are littered with bushes of thistles and thorns. All the days of your life you will toil, and no task will be made easy for you!"

God provided clothes for Adam and Eve, then led them away from the garden.

Beyond its boundaries, He knew that they would not be able to take from the Tree of Life, which would give them eternal life, as is so for God.

"When you have worked all the days of your life," said God, "Your bodies will return to dust, as it was from dust that you were made!"

Eve soon gave birth to two boys. The firstborn was called Cain, and to his brother, she gave the name Abel.

When they grew older, Cain and Abel worked the land for their parents. Cain grew crops, and tilled the soil. Abel looked after livestock, and became a diligent shepherd.

They both brought offerings from their labor to present to God. Cain brought fruits of the soil, while Abel brought fat calves and newly born lambs, that were the pride of his flock.

God was especially happy with Abel's gift, which made Cain feel angry and rejected.

God then spoke to Cain, asking him, "Why do you have such anger in your heart? If you do as I command, then you have no need to feel angry. But when you do not, your heart will be filled with hatred, and this will lead to your own destruction!"

Cain continued to be angry, feeling jealous toward his brother for the favor that God had shown to him.

The elder of the two sons burned with rage. And so it was that, when they were both in the fields together, Cain came upon his brother, catching him by surprise, and killing him.

God then summoned Cain, and challenged him, "Where now is your brother, my son, Abel?"

"I do not know!" Cain replied. "Am I the keeper of my brother?"

God knew that Cain was lying, for He knows everything that comes to pass.

"The land is stained with your brother's blood!" roared God. "With your own hands, you have taken away the life of your brother! For this, the land that is stained with the blood that is on your hands will no longer provide for you. No more will you reap abundant crops, but will now wander from place to place, ever in search of food and a place to rest!"

Cain prostrated himself before God. "My Great LORD!" he screamed, "This is too much for me to bear! I will never find peace, and as I wander, I will surely be set upon by strangers and be killed!"

Yet God promised Cain, "This will not be so! Anyone who kills you will face My wrath, and their punishment will be seven times greater than that which you must now endure."

Cain then began to wander the land, eventually coming to a place to the east of the garden, which is known as Nod. He married, and his wife bore a son, whose name was Enoch.

Enoch in turn married also, and his offspring grew, forming the next of a line of generations that take us to the time of Noah, when a great flood of water came upon the land (but that is a story for another day).

Adam and Eve also had another son, whose name was Seth. He too began a line of many generations, and saw his father live to a great age.

By the time Adam and Eve died, many of their descendants had again started turning back to trusting God. Yet they had traveled far from the original garden, and the life of beauty and perfection that God had once provided for them.

Our journeys through our own lives may sometimes be difficult, like those of Adam and Eve. But we should never forget that if we work hard, and are faithful to God, we may one day find our way back to the life of having only good things, as God wants for us.

We are all His children, and He longs for us to live in harmony with Him.

CHAPTER TWO

The Story of Noah and his Ark

MANY, MANY YEARS AGO–almost as long as history goes –there once lived an old man named Noah.

Noah had three sons, one of whom was at times fond of causing mischief. Still, Noah loved his family dearly, but his greatest love was for God.

Every day, Noah would wander to a place where he could be alone to talk with God. He told Him about his problems and concerns, about what he hoped for, and what pleased him, and what he wanted to thank God for.

Noah also prayed for his family and his friends, and for all the people of his village and homeland. He prayed for the animals, and thanked God for all the bright colors that he saw around him–the gentle flowers that open their petals to the golden sunlight, the bouncing jewels of white that glisten on the bobbing water of the river, and the endless sparkling of stars that shine brightly in the night sky.

Noah was very thankful, and had much joy in his heart. He listened to God, Who spoke clearly to him, and Noah promised to do whatever God asked of him.

One day, God called Noah and told him to warn his friends, and all the people of the village and his homeland, that God was very sorry that so few people were like Noah. No one else came to speak to Him every day as Noah did, and none would listen to what God wanted them to do.

In fact, many of Noah's friends thought that he was wasting his time talking with God. They enjoyed themselves, making merry in the village, sometimes causing mischief, and each pretending that they were more important and deserving of attention than others.

They bought more and more things to keep in their houses, which they thought would make them happy. Some argued among themselves, and even started to fight. They weren't always loving towards their families, and they did many things that upset God very much. Soon, many started to forget God's love for them, and they turned away from loving Him.

Since God loved everyone very deeply, the people's disobedience made him very upset. Noah too was very troubled by what he saw. Encouraged by God, Noah started to spend more and more of his time pleading with the people to remember God, and to have love for Him in their hearts.

Although he tried very hard to persuade them, no one would listen to Noah. When he spoke with his friends about God being angry with them, they just laughed at him, and told him to go away.

God was very sorry to see that the people whom He loved and whose very lives were given by Him no longer wanted to be friends with Him. His heart was very troubled to see that His faithful friend Noah was treated so badly. And He saw that, even though Noah tried very hard to convince the people to stop giving their attention to all manner of things that God disliked, they were determined not to change their minds.

So one day God decided that He would not allow Noah to be laughed at any more. He would bring about a new start for the world, one in which only good and faithful people like Noah could live freely and happily with Him.

When Noah came to speak to God that day, God told him: "My dear faithful friend and servant, My heart is full of sadness to see you being laughed at all the time. I am going to bring a great flood of water upon all of the Earth. So deep will the waters be, that no one who lives on the land will come out of the flood alive.

"Not the people who live here, nor the animals will live. Only those who are faithful to Me, and who love their families and all the things that I love, will be saved. And I will save two of each of the many animals that live on the earth, so that each of their kind may be with a mate and begin their lives again."

When he heard this, Noah was very sad, but he knew that God had a great plan for him.

"Here is how I intend that you and your family, and each of the animals, will survive when I send the mighty waters upon the earth," said God.

"I want you to build a large ark, like a giant, sturdy boat, that will float on top of the water until I bring sunlight once more, and send the waters back into the rivers and the seas. This is what I promise you, My peace and safe protection until I bring you again to dry land.

"I will tell you how to build this ark, and show you where you will find the wood and other materials that you will need to make it from. Do not be concerned, for I will make clear exactly how big it will need to be."

Noah listened very carefully to what God told him, although he was at first unsure that he would be able to build such a magnificent ark, since it was something that he had never done before.

Still, he trusted that God would show him the way, and knew that with God's help, he could do anything.

God then told Noah to warn the people that a great flood was coming. Even now, God wanted to give all of those who had wandered away from him a chance to come back and receive His love once more.

"Tell the people that they will not be able to survive the flood," God instructed Noah. "Tell them that I will show My deep love for those who come back to Me, and I will forgive them for all the bad things that they have done. I will make peace with them, and I will protect and bring them to a place of safety, as I will do for you and your family."

Noah listened carefully to what God told him, and once more, wandered around the streets of his village and throughout his homeland, warning the people of what God had told him.

"You are quite mad!" said many of the people. "There has never before been a flood like the one that you say is coming. We will be safe in our houses if these great waters that you speak about start to come, and we have saved up all the food that we will need in our granaries and storerooms."

Many people were very rude to Noah. They mocked him more cruelly than they had before, and teased him endlessly about his wild suggestion.

In his daily conversations with God, Noah made known his sadness, and also told God how he felt cruelly treated and pushed aside by the people that he loved.

God told Noah not to be afraid, and assured him that He alone would always love Noah, and make sure that he came to no harm.

So Noah continued to warn the people about their fate while there was still time, even though they called him many names and continued to make fun of him.

God showed Noah where to fetch wood and other materials that he would need to make the ark. With his sons helping him, Noah set about the huge task of building this magnificent floating home. He sold his goods to pay for the materials, and was even ready to give up his own home, because he knew that when the flood came, the ark would be his only place of shelter, and his old house would be of no more use to him.

Soon, news of Noah's fantastic building project became widely known. People came by Noah's house to see whether what others had told them was true. When they saw Noah and his sons busily sawing wood and hammering nails into large beams of cedar and oak, they were sure that he had become quite mad, and laughed at him all the more.

"What a foolish man you are!" they shouted. "Who can believe your crazy story? There is no flood coming, and it will be you who has wasted so much time and money making such a ridiculous contraption!"

Still, Noah kept busily building the ark. Slowly, it began to take shape. God had told Noah that the ark should have three large rooms, organized on different decks. It was to have a very large door, with a ramp made of wood leading up to it, by which Noah and his family and all the animals could easily enter into the ark. Noah added a small window, and cut a small space in the roof of the ark, as God had instructed him.

When it was finished, the ark towered high above Noah's house. Still, there was no sign of rain. The people carried on laughing at Noah, although they were amazed at what he had built.

Even now, Noah continued to tell the people of the village that they could still be saved when the floods came if they turned back to loving God. But no one believed him, and none gave up their familiar ways.

God then told Noah that it was nearly time to enter the ark, but that first Noah should bring two of each of the different animals to the place where he had built the magnificent craft. He was then to allow them to enter into the ark. God promised to summon a pair of each of the animals that Noah could not find, such as the smallest insects, and the many different colored birds that fly in the air.

When all of the animals had come together, God told Noah that it was time to let them go into the ark, and then that he and his family should also follow them and wait for the rains to begin.

As God instructed, the animals marched in their pairs up the large wooden ramp that led to the door of the ark. Both female and male of every species made their way up the ramp, and for some types of animal, more than one pair came into the ark.

Leaping llamas and loveable labradors, elegant eagles and enormous elephants, pale-feathered pigeons and peculiar-looking porcupines, rarely-seen red raccoons and orange-bearded orangutans–animals of every kind entered into the ark, and then Noah and his family also followed on behind them.

When all were safely settled inside the ark, Noah secured shut the large door, and waited patiently for what God told him to do next.

One week after Noah closed the door of the ark, the rains began to fall. Dark clouds filled the skies, and lightning flashed all around. The rain beat down so heavily, that it was as though many furious waterfalls were pouring out of the sky. Soon, the ground was totally covered with water, and the streets became like rivers.

Then God made all the water that was underground come out onto the earth through many springs, and soon their water too collected into mighty rivers that rushed down into the village where Noah had lived.

The people of the village and the land all around now began to see that Noah's warning was not so foolish. They cried out to be saved, climbing onto the roofs of their houses as the waters began to rise higher and higher.

River after river burst its banks, causing the water to pour out onto the land. Soon, enough water covered the earth to allow the ark to float.

The people of the village climbed higher and higher as they ran to the hills, but the rains kept coming.

"Save us!" they cried out to Noah. "Let us come with you in your ark, now we see that we were wrong to make fun of you, and we are very sorry! We will always be faithful to God from this moment onward!"

But it was too late for them to be saved. The ark floated away from the village, and even when the people reached the very top of the hills that they were climbing, they could not escape the rising waters.

Soon, the whole Earth was covered with water. Not a single animal nor person that lived upon the Earth was saved. All were drowned in the dark, cold waters that swirled around and consumed them.

Some tried to escape in small fishing boats that had been moored on the riverside. But no boat other than the ark could stay afloat, as they were tossed by wave after wave that towered high into the sky.

While it bobbed up and down, the ark floated on the surface of the water, being guided to safety by God.

Noah and his family felt safe in God's care, although they were afraid to open the window of the ark to see what was happening outside. Noah and his sons had brought all the food that they would need into the ark, and so they huddled together, and gave thanks to God.

The floodwaters kept rising for many days, covering even the highest mountains. No creature could survive the flood that kept coming. No bird in the sky could withstand the terrible hurricanes and continual outpouring of rain that came from above.

For a full forty days and forty nights the water kept coming. Noah and his family wondered whether they might set foot on dry land again, but remembered that God had said that He would bring them to a place where they would be safe, and provide the food that they would need to eat.

After many months since the ark set sail, the waters finally started to dwindle. God stopped the rain from falling, and made the water from underground return to its tunnels and hidden caverns. He sent powerful winds to spread the waters far and wide, and He guided the ark to a place where it might rest.

Slowly, the water level began to fall. The tops of the mountains could be seen once more, and after a long time, the leafless branches of the tallest trees came into view.

God let the sun shine brightly upon the Earth once more, gently warming and comforting the faces of Noah, his family, and all the animals. The sun's warmth helped to dry the tops of the mountains, and dried the small patches of land that began to appear from under the endless waters.

The dark skies turned to the brightest blue, and Noah began to wonder whether it might finally be time to open the window of the ark.

Firstly, Noah decided to send a raven out from the ark, to see whether it might return, or fly away to feed on food that it had found floating on the water. The raven didn't return, so Noah realized that the water was calming.

Then, Noah sent out a dove, to see whether she too might return to him, or find a place where she might build her nest.

The first time he sent out the dove, she came back to him, landing gently on his hand. Noah reasoned that she could not find a place to build her nest, so he waited one more week, and then sent her out again.

Again, the dove returned, landing gently on Noah's hand. But this time, she returned to him with an olive branch, which Noah received with great hope, as he realized that the waters must be receding, and that God was showing that he would soon come to a place of safety. Noah accepted the olive branch as a symbol of God's peace and love, remembering that God had promised to protect Noah and his family.

Even now, the dove did not want to fly away, and the waters still covered much of the land, so Noah waited one more week before once again sending her out.

The third time that he set her free, the dove flew away, never to return to the ark again. Now Noah knew that dry land must be near. He waited a while longer, but knew that it would not be long before he and his family could again set foot on dry land.

Eventually, the ark rested itself upon firm ground, and very soon, the water had fallen away so much that Noah felt that it was time to open the large door and lower its ramp so that the animals could go back onto the land.

When the land was completely dry, Noah and his family also went out from the ark. They learned that the ark had rested on the top of a mountain, one of the tallest mountains called Ararat, and that this was the place from which they would venture forth to start the new world, as God had promised.

Noah was full of thanks to God for bringing him and his family to safety.

"I always trusted you, my dear Lord!" said Noah, and he set about building an altar to God, and then offering many prayers of thanks to Him.

God saw what Noah was doing, and loved him all the more for the love that he showed to Him.

"Nevermore will I bring such a flood upon the Earth," God promised, "For I love my people, and I see that you love me too."

To help Noah and his family, and all those who were born after them, to remember His promise, God set a rainbow in the sky. Its bright colors reflected the sun's light that God had sent after the rains, and its wide arch reminded Noah that God's love reaches over every obstacle that might seem to stand in the way.

"Whenever you see a rainbow, remember that I love you and will never leave you alone," said God.

And so it is today that whenever we see a rainbow, we can remember that God loves us too. This is what Noah also did, and he and his family lived happily in God's care for many, many more years after the ark finally brought them safely to dry land.

Let us be thankful to God for all that He gives us. He, we know, can always be trusted!

CHAPTER THREE

Abraham, The Man who was Faithful to God

AFTER THE ARK he built had settled on dry land, Noah had many descendants. Nine full generations passed. Then, a boy named Abram was born to a man called Terah.

Abram had two brothers, one of whom had a son called Lot, who we shall meet later in our story. When the time came for him to marry, Abram was overjoyed to be joined with a beautiful girl named Sarai, whose beauty was celebrated by all who knew her.

Terah moved his family and all their possessions from place to place, so that they could find water and graze their animals, until they came at last to the place where he was born, which also came to be the place where he would pass on from this life.

Abram always listened very carefully to God, and obeyed what He told him to do.

When his father died, God told Abram to leave his father's hometown, taking his family and all of his possessions with him. God promised Abram that He would provide much land for him, and bless him with many children and grandchildren.

Abram never doubted God's word, and gave thanks to Him wherever he set up his camp.

Abram led his camels along rocky mountain paths and over barren plains. Together with his nephew Lot, and his family too, this faithful family roamed from place to place in search of water, often pitching their tents in the wildest and most unwelcoming of places.

Yet Abram always remembered to thank God for bringing him and his family to a place of safety. And God often reminded Abram that He would bless him with a legacy that would become known throughout the world.

"My dear Abram, I will make you the leader of a powerful nation," said God. "You will be the father of so many offspring, that you will not be able to count them all!"

Living in the desert was not easy. Very little rain came, and there was little food for Abram and his family to eat. So, they kept walking until they came to the land of Egypt, where a mighty river flowed, which was able to support all kinds of life, and provided water so that plants and trees could grow.

Abram knew that the ruler of Egypt, or Pharaoh as he was known, would want to make Sarai his wife, because she was very beautiful. Fearing that his life may be in danger because of this, Abram suggested to Sarai that she make herself known to be his sister.

Pharaoh soon got to hear about Sarai's great beauty, and asked that she be brought into his palace to live with him. As a favor to Abram, Pharaoh gave many gifts and livestock for him to tend, but took Sarai into his palace, as though she were his own wife.

God was angry with what He saw, and brought a great plague upon the country. Many people died, and even Pharaoh feared for his own life. When he questioned why the plagues were happening, someone who knew the truth about Sarai told him that this beautiful woman was really Abram's wife.

Pharaoh was furious to receive this news, but wishing the plagues to end, ordered Sarai to return to her husband, and for them to quickly leave the country.

Knowing that Pharaoh would come after him if he stayed in Egypt, Abram once again set off with his family, his many camels, and grazing animals. The party traveled many miles, until they came again to the rocky mountain paths and barren plains that they had left behind many years before.

Lot, his family, and the herdspeople who looked after his animals left Egypt with Abram too. But the land that they came to was too dry to grow any crops, and there were too few fields where they might graze their goats and sheep.

Soon, arguments broke out among Abram and Lot's farmhands about who had the right to graze their animals on this particular piece of land or that. Lot and Abram both loved God and always sought to make peace in any dispute, but many of those who followed them did not.

With so many mouths to feed, Abram spoke with Lot, and suggested that they might separate, so that they might settle in different places where there might be a better chance for them to survive.

"My dear friend and nephew Lot," began Abram. "While it is hard for me to see you go, now is the time that we should settle in our own lands. Choose which you prefer, to the east or to the west, and I will take my family the opposite way!"

Lot knew that the land to the west was much easier for farming. There was a lively river there, and a sea filled with fish. Many trees and grasses grew there because of the water that the river and sea provided. So Lot chose to take his family into this green and fertile place, while Abram tended lands elsewhere.

At that time were many kings who claimed the same lands for themselves. After a time, some kings grouped together to fight their rivals. It was following one victory in this bitter war that Lot and his family were themselves captured, and taken as prisoners by the victorious army.

A messenger who had seen what had happened managed to escape to tell Abram all that he had seen.

Abram felt great love for his nephew, and so resolved to rescue him from this terrible situation.

Quickly, Abram gathered a strong force of men, and set out to find his nephew.

When they came upon the place where Lot was being held, Abram split his army into small groups. With one party, he came by night in a raid, rescuing Lot and all his family. So clever was Abram in his attack, and so tired were his enemy's troops after many years of fighting, that Abram was able to conquer more land too, killing the very king who had taken Lot prisoner.

The king of Sodom pleaded with Abram to return the people to his land, but Abram refused. Yet still, Abram offered the defeated king one tenth of all his animals and other possessions.

God spoke to Abram often, and Abram never failed to give thanks to God for all that He had given him.

One night, God spoke to Abram in one of his dreams, telling him that he would become the father of a great nation.

"Come with me," said God. "Step outside your tent and see the millions of twinkling stars that shine in the sky!

"As many will be your descendants than the number of stars that you can count there!"

"From the great river in Egypt to the fast-flowing Euphrates in the east, all these vast lands I will give to you!"

Abram did not doubt God, although he did not know how such a wonder as for his wife to fall pregnant could come to be, because his wife Sarai had been unable to bear him a child.

Still, Abram trusted God, and believed what He told him, that his descendants would number as many as the stars! God promised to always protect and love Abram's children as His own, and Abram in turn made a promise to God to always be faithful to Him.

Sarai knew that her husband longed for a child, and so she proposed to him that he take her slave girl Hagar to be a mother for his child. Abram agreed with this plan, and through Hagar, a son was soon to be born, who would be called Ishmael.

Hagar was distraught when she became pregnant, for she learned that this was Sarai's plan. She felt cruelly cheated, and began to dislike her mistress, to whom until then she had always been faithful.

In turn, Sarai became angry at the girl, pulling her hair, calling her names, and making her do all sorts of terrible jobs.

Sarai's punishments caused Hagar to become afraid, and she cried in her bed every night. Eventually, she decided that she could no longer stay in Abram's household, and so she ran away, although with no idea about where she might go.

God loved Hagar, as He loves everyone, and He sent one of His angels to comfort her.

The angel found Hagar crouched beside a well. Terrified and alone, Hagar knew that she might drink water here to refresh her dry and trembling body.

"Dear child!" started the angel. "Why are you weeping? God loves you, and it is His Will that you will give birth to a son, whose name will be Ishmael.

"Do not be afraid. You must return to your mistress and serve her well. Your son will be wild in nature, and he will be taunted by many people. But God will one day make him leader of a great nation, and many generations will come after him. Believe this, dear Hagar, because God loves you and it is His wish that you love Him too!"

Hagar, while trembling, trusted what the angel told her. Filled with love in her heart, she promised to return to her mistress, and to be a good mother to Ishmael. She cried out to God, who answered her, "My dear child, you see Me." The place where Hagar heard God is called Beer-lahai-roi, which means , "the well of him that lives and sees Me."

Abram welcomed Hagar back into his camp, and promised to be a good father to her son when her baby was born.

Soon after, God spoke again to Abram, telling him that from that moment on that he was to be known as "Abraham". God desired a new name for Sarai too, and she became known as "Sarah".

Abraham loved his new son Ishmael, but he wished that his wife Sarah could also bear him an heir.

One day, while Abraham was sitting under the shade of the canopy of his tent to cool himself during the heat of the day, three travelers passed by. Abraham called out to them, beckoning them to stay awhile and be his guests. He asked Sarah to bake cakes for them and ordered a servant boy to fetch a calf that might be prepared for their supper. Abraham felt certain that these men were close to God.

The visitors gratefully accepted Abraham's hospitality, and knew that he was a good man. One of the men, who was really a messenger of God's, assured Abraham that Sarah would soon give birth to a son. His conversation could be heard by Sarah, who was sitting in her tent nearby.

Now, Sarah and Abraham were already very old, much older than is normal to have children. Sarah doubted that she could ever give birth, for she had not been so blessed until now. So when she overheard the words that were spoken to Abraham, she laughed out loud.

One of Abraham's visitors questioned why his wife was laughing, as he declared that nothing was impossible for God. Then Sarah became afraid, and she pretended that she had taken what she had heard seriously.

What the visitors had promised came to be-within one year, Sarah had a son, who was given the name Isaac. Sarah laughed with joy, amazed and very happy that God had performed such a miracle at her advanced age. And so Isaac was raised by a mother who was much older than most people we may ever know!

Before they departed after their supper, the visitors joined Abraham for a walk. As they walked, they spoke about the sad situation of the city of Sodom, where Abraham's nephew Lot was now living, along with its near neighbor, the city of Gomorrah.

"Such wicked people inhabit these cities," lamented Abraham, "Except for my dear nephew Lot. How far they have turned away from God, no longer loving Him, nor doing what pleases Him. My heart is broken to see what they have become. So much lying and cheating, stealing and hurting one another. They have no respect for God, nor for each other!"

The visitors revealed what God had in mind for these wicked people, for God saw that they would never turn back to loving him.

"In a very short time," said one, "God will destroy these very places. He will tear apart their houses, and bring molten rocks tumbling down upon them. The fire will burn so strongly, that not even a single brick will remain as a reminder of the cities that were once there. Every building and every person that remains will be completely buried under ash and brimstone, for a terrible firestorm is coming upon them."

Upon hearing these words, Abraham was very troubled. He fell to his knees and pleaded with God that He might save anyone there who was faithful to Him.

"My dear God, will You not spare the lives of Your people, if there are but fifty in these cities who will turn to You?"

"Certainly I will save them!" promised God.

"Then what if there are only forty, or thirty, or even twenty good people living there?" asked Abraham, "Will you still save them?"

"You hear my promise that I will," answered God.

"What if there are fewer still, no more than ten who will honor You?" continued Abraham, "Will you still show mercy for them?"

"If there are only ten found in those cities who have love for Me," replied God, "I will not bring them to harm."

Abraham then returned to his tent, and two of the visitors set upon the path to Sodom, where they might see for themselves how many people loved God.

When they entered through one of the large gates of the city, they were sighted by Lot, who beckoned them to join him in his house, where he would be pleased to entertain them as his guests.

The men at first refused, but Lot was insistent. They then joined him for a fine supper, knowing that Lot was a good man.

While they ate, a large group gathered outside Lot's house, berating him to bring his visitors outside, such that they may do with them as they will.

Fearing for his guests' safety, Lot refused their request, but instead offered his own daughters to be taken by the crowd, even though they had not yet come to full maturity. The chiding crowd still called out for the men inside.

Seeing that it was Lot's deep love and desire to be a perfect host for strangers that drove him to make this offer, the men pulled him back into his house just as the crowd attempted to break down his door. With God's power, those who were gathered outside were blinded, so that they could no longer find their way to Lot's door.

Early next morning, the visitors warned Lot that he must immediately gather his family and flee from the city, for God was soon to completely destroy it.

"You must go right away without delay," begged the men, "There is no time to waste! Run to the hills, but do not turn around to look back at the city."

Lot hesitated for a moment, but the visitors grabbed both him and his wife by their hands, and quickly led them out of the city, urging them and their family to make haste in fleeing to a place of safety.

"Remember, do not turn back to see what is here!" they warned.

No sooner had they left the city, than a great ball of fire fell upon Sodom, and also upon its neighbor, the city of Gomorrah. Poisonous, black smoke towered into the sky, higher and thicker than the smoke that rises up from any furnace.

Burning rocks poured down upon the buildings, crushing everyone below them. When the firestorm stopped, not a trace of any person or any thing could be seen. But still the smoke could be seen for many miles around, billowing high into the sky for many days and nights.

Lot had fled as the men encouraged, resting first at a town some distance away, which the men had told him would provide a safe haven for him. But his wife ignored the men's warning, turning around to look once more at the city and the life that she loved. As she did so, in an instant, she was turned into a pillar of salt!

The following morning, Abraham looked toward where Sodom and Gomorrah had once been, where not even ten good men had been found. But Abraham heard that his nephew was safe, and bowed down and gave thanks to God.

"My faithful child Lot never deserted Me," said God, "And I never will turn away from him. Anyone who loves Me will live, and be safe in the protection of My perfect love."

Abraham was overjoyed to hear this, and loved God and his nephew Lot all the more.

Abraham had set up his camp in the land of the Philistines. Thinking this people to be disloyal toward God, and feeling that he might be despised for being married to such a beautiful wife, Abraham made it widely known that Sarah was his sister, as he had done before when he came to Egypt.

As had Pharaoh before him, the king of the land, who was called Abimelech, sent for Sarah to join him in his household, where he planned to make her his wife. Yet God came to him in a dream, warning him that he must not marry Sarah, because she was already married to Abraham.

Troubled by his dream, the king questioned why God would also protect Abraham and his people, when he had seemed to deceive him by naming Sarah as his sister. God told him that He did indeed protect Abraham, who was a good man, and that the king must allow Sarah to return to him.

When they met again, Abraham explained to Abimelech that he had not lied to him. Not only was Sarah his wife, but she was also his half-sister. And this was true. Abimelech prostrated himself before Abraham, begging for his forgiveness for doubting his integrity. He promised Abraham that he could settle wherever he wished in his land, also offering him precious gifts and many livestock to add to his own.

Abraham made peace with the king, and thanked him for his apology and gifts. Abraham also prayed for Abimelech and his people, asking God that he would bless the many women in the land with children, for until then very few had fallen pregnant.

Abraham remained in the king's land, but another dispute arose between them over who had dug a deep well. Abraham then offered animals and swore an oath that this had been his doing, and the two men again agreed to live in peace.

Now Ishmael, Abraham's son who had been raised by Hagar, had taken to teasing his younger brother Isaac, which greatly troubled Sarah. Because of his mischief and constant insults towards his brother, Sarah told Ishmael that he should not inherit the family's title. This she insisted to Abraham, although he deeply loved his son. Wondering what he should do, Abraham prayed to God, who told him to follow Sarah's advice, and so he sent Ishmael and his mother away from the camp.

Hagar and Ishmael wandered for many miles in the wilderness, soon emptying the bottle of water and devouring the bread that Abraham had given to them when they parted. Falling to the ground in tears, and desperate for water to quench her thirst, Hagar cried out to The Lord.

"My God, why have you brought me such misery?" cried Hagar. "Surely, my life must now be over, and that of my son besides?"

Hearing her crying, God sent an angel to speak to her and to give her hope.

"Dear child," said the angel. "Do not be afraid, for your God loves you. Your son will become a great man, and a leader of many people. God will not let you die in the wilderness, but will provide for what you need."

At that moment, Ishmael and Hagar saw that a wellspring had appeared before them, and so they took water and gave thanks to God.

As he grew older, Ishmael's strength increased, and he became very skilled as an archer. In time, he was married, and had many offspring, just as the angel had assured his mother.

Meantime, Abraham's younger son Isaac was growing, but was still a boy.

God decided to test Abraham's love for Him, and this is how He decided this test.

God told Abraham to take Isaac to a mountain many miles away, where he was to build an altar and sacrifice his own son upon it. God knew that if Abraham would be ready to give up the life of his own son for His sake, then Abraham's pure love for God would be proven.

Abraham was very troubled when he heard what God commanded him to do, but did not waver in his faithfulness. Taking his son with him, he wandered for many miles, making for a mountain that God had directed him to.

"Where are we going, my father?" asked Isaac, as they ventured further away from the camp.

"Do not be afraid," replied Abraham, "We are going where God wants us to be."

"What will be your sacrifice?" asked Isaac, seeing that his father had gathered wood, ready to start a fire for a burnt offering.

"God will provide the lamb," his father resolutely replied.

When they arrived at the mountaintop that God had led them to, Abraham set about the task of building an altar. He took Isaac in his arms, and laid him on the wood that he had set down there, ready to make his sacrifice to God, as God had commanded him to.

Abraham raised his knife ready to take his son's life. Now God knew that Abraham would always be faithful to Him. Before he could bring his hand down, God sent an angel to stop Abraham from sacrificing Isaac. Then He showed him a ram that was caught by its horns in a thicket nearby, which he might offer as a sacrifice instead.

"Now I know that your love is beyond any doubt!" said God. "You are truly worthy to be the father of a great nation, and for your loyalty to Me, I will give you yet more lands and pour out many blessings upon you!"

Abraham lived for many more years, seeing his son Isaac married to a beautiful girl named Rebecca, and even living long enough to see the birth of a pair of grandson twins, Esau and Jacob, who themselves went on to be ancestors of what God promised would be a great nation.

When he died, Abraham was buried alongside his wife Sarah, who had passed away some years before him. Both of his sons, Isaac and Ishmael, came to bury him, and both began the family lines of many, many people. As many in number as the twinkling stars that shine in the sky would follow them, as God had promised.

As God always keeps His promises, Abraham's family line still continues to this day.

CHAPTER FOUR
Joseph and his Brothers

DURING THE EARLY DAYS when people first lived on the earth, there lived a man named Jacob, who, with his first wife Leah, made their home in a land known as Canaan. Jacob was soon to become known as "Israel" by God, because he was the father of twelve sons, who in turn came to be the leaders of twelve great tribes and family lines that survive to this day.

One of Jacob's younger sons was called Joseph, whom Jacob loved dearly, since he had been born to him in his old age. When he was old enough, Joseph joined his elder brothers in his father's fields, tending sheep, and helping in any way that he could.

However, Joseph's brothers were angry with him, for he often gave bad reports to his father about them, and the work that they left him to do. The brothers' anger turned to envy when Jacob decided to make a special gift for Joseph. This was a finely embroidered tunic, emblazoned with many different colors, and falling all the way to the floor. It was a magnificent sight–fit even for a prince, and Joseph wept tears of joy when his father gave him this gift, spending many hours sitting close by him, enjoying embraces with him. He loved his tunic so much, that he wore it almost all the time, proudly showing it off to his brothers and anyone who came nearby.

"Look at him!" cried his brothers. "Now he thinks that he is his father's favorite, and deserving of special favors. He must think that he is better than us, being worth more in his father's sight than all of us put together. We will show him that we will not be thought of as being less worthy than he!"

The brothers continued to fume and rant, while Joseph paraded around in his fine tunic, proudly showing off the beautiful gift that his father had given him to all who passed by.

One night, Joseph had a dream, which he shared with his brothers while they were working in the fields the next day.

"In my dream I saw that we were all working together binding sheaves," began Joseph. "The sheave that I was binding grew very tall, towering above those that were in your hands, which bowed down to it!"

Joseph's brothers were enraged when they heard this, believing that he was telling them that he planned to rule over them. They began to believe that he was not like one of them, and started to avoid being with him, and called him all sorts of names.

Joseph then had another dream, which he also told to his brothers, and to his father also.

In this dream, Joseph said that he had seen the sun and the moon bowing down to him! Now, the sun and the moon are sometimes said to be like a great father and a great mother, so when he told this to Jacob, even his father was furious with him, although he didn't doubt that Joseph was telling the truth.

However, his brothers became so angry that they began to consider ways of teaching Joseph a lesson. Soon, their plans turned toward thoughts of even doing away with him altogether, such that they would not have to hear his crazy claims any more.

While they were working some fields many miles from their father's home, the brothers saw Joseph approaching them from a distance, and decided to carry out their terrible threat there and then.

"Here we can do away with him," said one of the brothers. "If we throw his body into the large pit that has been dug on the edge of this field to collect water, we can tell our father that he was killed by a wild animal on his way to find us. The old man will never know the truth!"

However, one of the brothers, whose name was Reuben, said that it was wrong to kill Joseph.

"We do not need to have blood on our hands," he pleaded with the other brothers. "We can capture him, and leave him in the pit where no one will find him. That way, he will be left to face his own fate, whether he is helped by his dreams or not!"

Reuben secretly planned to rescue Joseph from the pit once he was alone from his brothers, but he did not make his plan known to anyone.

When Joseph approached them, his brothers pounced on him as they had planned, binding his hands and legs. They tore his precious tunic from him, and threw him into the pit.

"No more will you trouble us with your stupid dreams!" they said. "Now we will see who will grow taller over the others!"

The brothers then walked away from the pit, and settled down to have their lunch.

As they were eating, they noticed a long caravan of camels with their owners approaching them. These were travelers, who were passing by on their way to sell precious goods in a foreign country.

"See these rich merchants approaching us!" cried Judah, one of the brothers. "Why don't we sell our dear little brother, make some money for ourselves, and at the same time be done with him for good?"

"What a perfect plan!" The brothers replied. "Let him be a slave in a faraway land. That way, we me never hear from him again!"

So it was that the brothers' treacherous deal with the passing travelers was done, and Joseph was sold into slavery. In time, the merchants came to the land of Egypt, where he became the slave of Potiphar, who was captain of the guard of Pharaoh, the ruler of the land.

Reuben was not with his brothers when they made this deal, and he was distraught when he saw that Joseph had disappeared from the pit.

"What now shall we tell our father about the fate of his beloved son?" bemoaned Reuben. "How can we account for not looking after him while he was among our company?"

"That is easy!" replied one of the other brothers. "All we need do is dip his tunic in the blood of an animal, which we may show to our father, claiming that we found the torn and bloodied robe along our path, assuming that some wild animal had set upon our dear brother!"

"What an ingenious idea!" agreed the brothers. And so it was that they returned to their father carrying Joseph's tunic, which they had first soaked in the blood of a goat that they had killed.

"Dear father, we fear that we bring you terrible news!" they announced, when they arrived at their father's home.

"As we were returning from working in your fields, we came upon this robe, covered in blood, and fear that it may be the very same one that you gave to our dear brother Joseph!"

They handed the tunic to Jacob, who examined it closely, then let out a terrible cry.

"Without doubt, this is my dear son's tunic!" hollered Jacob. "He must have been killed by a wild animal as he was making his way to see you. My dear son is gone, and I am overcome with grief!"

Jacob wailed out loud, and could not be offered any comfort by his family. So dearly did he love his son, so pained was he to consider that they would never enjoy each other's embraces again.

Meantime in Egypt, Joseph worked diligently in his new role as Potiphar's slave. God never left him, and blessed him in everything that he did. So it was, that soon his master noticed how well Joseph worked, and how everything he turned his hands to prospered. In the household, he became very useful, and in the fields, rich harvests could be enjoyed because of his careful skill and attention. Soon, Potiphar came to see that Joseph was deeply blessed by God, and so he entrusted more and more responsibilities to him, even making him in charge of his household.

Joseph was very handsome, and Potiphar's wife longed to spend time with him alone.

"Come be with me, while my husband is away!" she pleaded to Joseph. "Let me pretend to be your wife for awhile, and do with me what you will!"

"I will have nothing to do with your plan!" replied Joseph, "For I cannot act wrongly against your husband, who is a good master to me. A husband and wife should be faithful to each other, and I cannot deceive the one who is your true husband."

Potiphar's wife continued to urge Joseph to change his mind, but he steadfastly refused.

One time, Joseph found himself to be alone in the house with her, when no other servants were around. She grabbed at his cloak, begging him to stay with her. But as he always did, he refused, and made quickly for the exit. However, Potiphar's wife kept hold of his cloak, which she took from him. Later that day, she protested to her husband that Joseph had attempted to approach her while she was sleeping, even leaving behind his cloak, which she was still holding.

Potiphar was furious with Joseph when he heard the story, believing his wife's account of what had happened.

"I have entrusted you with looking after my household, and managing all the workers in my field, and you repay me by wanting to trouble my wife!" hollered Potiphar. "For this, you must surely be punished!"

Without allowing Joseph an opportunity to present his side of the story, Potiphar commanded that he be thrown into Pharaoh's dungeons, where he might cause no more trouble.

God remained close to Joseph while he languished in his cold, dark cell, with its muddy puddles, scurrying rats, and creeping creatures of many kinds.

"Why have you put me here?" protested Joseph. "What now is my destiny? You alone know that I have done no wrong!"

God heard Joseph's cry, and spoke to him in a powerful, but kind voice.

"Do not be afraid! I will never leave you alone, My son," promised God. "Wait, and you will see that you are soon as valued here as you once were by your last master!"

Knowing that God was by his side, Joseph prayed very diligently, and the calm and peace that surrounded him soon persuaded the prison warder to put him in charge of jobs that were reserved only for trusted prisoners. As he had while directing the work in the fields and in the household of his old master, Joseph succeeded in every task that he was given, soon winning over the full trust of the prison warder.

After a while, two new prisoners were entrusted to Joseph's care. These were the chief cupbearer and head baker of Pharaoh, who had both offended their master. Both men were attended to by Joseph, and soon came to know him well.

It happened one night that both men had vivid dreams. The following morning, Joseph came to them and saw that they were both troubled.

"What causes you such distress?" asked Joseph.

"We both have had strange dreams," they replied, "But we don't know the meaning that they hold for us. Please lead us to someone who can interpret their purpose."

Joseph announced that he could interpret the dreams for the men, and so each in turn told him what they had been shown.

The cupbearer related his story first.

"In my dream, I saw a grapevine that had three branches. These grew to full height, and beautiful grapes blossomed on them. I had Pharaoh's cup in my hand, and so I squeezed the grapes into this, allowing it to be filled with precious wine. Then I handed the cup to Pharaoh."

"I have heard you," answered Joseph. "And this is what your dream means. The three branches that you saw represent three days. After this time, Pharaoh will release you from this prison and take you back into his charge as his cupbearer, just as you once were."

"I beseech you to remember me, your servant Joseph, when Pharaoh deals kindly with you. Tell him of my plight, that I may also be released, for I was imprisoned here unfairly for a crime that I did not commit!"

The cupbearer promised to remember Joseph when he was again in Pharaoh's service, but in fact, he quickly put Joseph out of his mind when Joseph's prophecy came to be true.

Then the baker, believing that since the cupbearer's dream had had such a fortuitous meaning, that his would too, started to relate what had come to him during the night.

"In my dream," began the baker, "I saw that I was carrying three baskets filled with bread upon my head. The top basket was filled with the choicest pastries, which were intended for Pharaoh, but many birds were pecking away at its delicious contents."

"Your dream has the following meaning," responded Joseph. "Following three days, Pharaoh will decree that your head should be cut off from your body. Then your body will be hauled onto a giant pole. There, the wild birds will tear at your flesh, and leave your bones to be devoured by wild animals!"

Unfortunately for the baker, after three days, Joseph's prediction came to be true. Pharaoh refused to grant the baker a pardon, instead insisting that he be put to death!

These two men were not alone in having dreams. Pharaoh himself had two dreams that troubled him deeply.

In the first dream, Pharaoh saw himself standing beside the great River Nile. There, he watched while seven healthy and fat cows came out of the water and began grazing among the reeds along the riverbank. Next, seven very unhealthy looking, thin cows emerged from the river's fast-flowing water. Immediately, the seven thin cows swallowed up the seven healthy cows that were in front of them.

Pharaoh's second dream showed seven ears of corn that were growing on one side of a single stalk. These appeared ripe for picking, lively and blossoming. Then, seven other ears of corn appeared. These were dark in color and poorly formed, scorched by the sun's heat. Yet these feeble-looking ears of corn swallowed up the healthy ones. This was the strangest sight that Pharaoh had ever seen!

When he woke, Pharaoh summoned his trusted advisors and wise men, whom he hoped could explain the meaning of these strange dreams. Yet none was able to do so. Pharaoh's cupbearer stood close by while the men deliberated, who was at once reminded of the interpretation of his own dream that he had been given by Joseph.

"My Glorious Majesty, I beg you to grant me an opportunity to speak!" petitioned the cupbearer. "While I was in prison, I met a Hebrew man who was once a slave of your captain of the guard. This man dealt kindly with me, listening carefully to me when I had been troubled by a strange dream. He interpreted the dream for me, and within three days, what he told me would happen came to be."

Desperate to help him understand the meaning of the dreams that were causing him such worry, Pharaoh immediately ordered that Joseph be brought before him. Pharaoh then relayed his dreams to Joseph, exactly as he had told them to his advisors and wise men.

"Your Majesty, with God's help, I can explain the meaning of these dreams," began Joseph. "In fact, the two dreams have the same meaning. The seven healthy cows and seven healthy ears of corn represent seven years of prosperity which are to come, when there will be rich harvests and great abundance in the land. The seven unhealthy cows and weak ears of corn represent seven terrible years of famine that will then follow.

"Unless your majesty heeds this warning, making provision for those years of want to come while the harvest is plentiful, your people and their animals will surely die.

"Allow me to suggest that the grain that is harvested during the time of plenty should be well managed. Let some be kept aside in store, such that there will be sufficient food to eat when the famine arrives."

Pharaoh was grateful for Joseph's interpretation, believing that God had spoken to him. Furthermore, he saw that Joseph was a wise and capable man, a suitable steward to be put in charge of the task of ensuring that the kingdom's grain stocks were well managed during the time of plenty, and allocated wisely during the years of need.

And so it was that Joseph was appointed chief steward by Pharaoh, responsible for overseeing the management of all the land of Egypt. None other than Pharaoh himself had such power.

Joseph wore the most elaborate finery, and traveled from place to place in a magnificent chariot that Pharaoh ordered to be made for him. Joseph was married to Asenath, the daughter of a priest, and he became celebrated throughout the land.

Two sons were born to Joseph and his wife, and Joseph lived happily, thanking God for always being by his side.

During the seven years of prosperity, Joseph did as he had advised Pharaoh. He made sure that vast quantities of grain from what was harvested were held back, such that food would be available when the years of suffering came. And so it was, that after seven profitable years, seven years of hardship began. Little rain fell, and no crops could grow. All over Egypt, and in other nations too, the land produced no crops to feed the people, and many people were soon starving.

Pharaoh told his people to obey what Joseph told them to do. As the famine spread more widely, Joseph allowed the storehouses to be opened, and grain was sold to those in need. Not just to the Egyptians, but others traveled from afar, willing to pay a high price for grain, for their people too were starving.

Among those who came were ten men from Canaan, who were the ten elder brothers of Joseph. Joseph's younger brother, who was called Benjamin, stayed with his father, who feared for his safety.

The brothers came before Joseph in his richly furnished palace, and bowed low before him.

"Mighty Lord!" they began. "We have come from a faraway land, where our father and all our family are starving, hoping that you may allow us to buy a little of your grain, which we will pay for with these bags of silver."

The brothers then presented ten bags filled with silver, expecting Joseph to honor their request. They did not recognize their own brother, but Joseph immediately saw that they were his own kin.

"I do not believe that you have come here to buy grain!" Joseph roughly responded, wishing to test his brothers. "I say that you are spies, and that you have come to learn secrets about our land!"

"Our Lord, this is not so!" pleaded the brothers. "We have left our elderly father and his youngest son at home. This son he loves dearly, as he lost one other. Were we not to return to him with food as we promised, we will all surely die!"

"I will hear none of this!" barked Joseph, speaking carefully, so as not to give away his true identity. "If you are not spies, then send one from among you to bring me this younger brother that you speak about. The rest of you will be confined in my prison until the one you claim you left behind is brought to me!"

Joseph then ordered that the men be seized and thrown into the dungeon. But after three days, he decreed that just one of them might be kept captive, while the others were sent on their way with grain, and a warning that the brother who was being held as a ransom would not be released unless the others returned with their younger brother.

Unbeknown to the brothers, Joseph had also instructed his servants to place the bags of silver back into the baskets of grain that they now carried with them. Joseph had overheard his brothers speaking in Hebrew about him, although since they did not recognize him, they did not know that their words could be understood by him.

"This must be punishment for the way that we treated our brother, Joseph!" whispered the brothers among themselves. "I told you that we should not deal so roughly with the boy," complained Reuben, "But you would not listen. Now we must all face punishment for what happened!"

After he overheard what his brothers had said, Joseph retreated to a place where he could be alone, where he wept bitterly. Despite the way that they had treated him, Joseph loved his brothers, and longed to be reunited with his father and his younger brother, Benjamin.

The men set off on their way back to Canaan, discovering before long that the bags of silver that they had presented to Joseph had been returned in the baskets of grain that they were carrying.

"Surely our lives will not be spared for this!" lamented the brothers. "The Lord of Egypt will believe that we secreted this money before we departed his palace, and he will surely believe us to be thieves as well as spies!"

After a long journey, the brothers arrived back in the land of Canaan, and came before their father. They told him all that had happened in Egypt, including Joseph's insistence that Benjamin be taken to see him.

"How wretched am I!" exclaimed Jacob. "My son Joseph was taken from me, and now another languishes in a prison in Egypt. Now you want me to give up my dear son Benjamin, who is my comfort and my joy!"

"Dear father," offered Reuben. "I vow to you that you can take the lives of my own two dear sons if we do not return from Egypt with Benjamin. You have my word that we will care for him with the same love that you have for him!"

Jacob was beside himself, continuing to insist that he would not allow Benjamin to leave his side. But the famine worsened, and so it again became necessary for the brothers to consider traveling to Egypt to buy more grain.

This time, another of the brothers, Judah, promised Jacob that he would guard Benjamin with his life. Seeing that their situation was desperate, Jacob finally agreed to allow Benjamin to travel with them. He sent them off with gifts for Joseph (he did not know that the man who was described as being the chief governor of Egypt was in fact his own son). He entrusted to his sons ten more bags of silver to pay for the grain, warning them that the other money that was put into their baskets must also be returned.

Finally, he prayed for their safety, kissed each one of them in turn, and gave them his blessing.

The brothers made a swift path to Egypt, praying that they might quickly receive an audience with Joseph. When Joseph heard that his brothers had returned, he ordered that a fine feast be prepared for them.

In fear for their lives, the brothers owned up to the servant of Joseph about the silver that they had found in their bags when they last departed for their homeland. They suggested that this may have happened by mistake, and offered at once to return the bags, along with an equal number with which to buy new grain.

The servant assured them that their honesty meant that no harm would come to them, and let them prepare to meet Joseph in his private quarters for the feast.

Sitting at a table apart from them, as was the custom, Joseph welcomed the returning travelers. Seeing Benjamin among them, he enquired, "Is this the younger brother that you spoke about?"

The men confirmed that this was so.

Then Joseph said, "You are blessed, my son," before instructing the feast to be served. Joseph even allowed food to be served directly from his own table, with the largest portion being offered to Benjamin.

Joseph was filled with both love and sadness, for he wanted to embrace his brothers, but the time was not yet right to make his identity known. So he escaped for a while to a private room, where he was able to weep openly, before washing his face and returning to his table.

The following morning, the brothers prepared to leave for their home. However, Joseph gave instructions to his servants as before, ordering them to hide the silver that his brothers had brought with them in the baskets of grain that they would carry back to their father.

"Put not just the silver coins," instructed Joseph, "But also my very own cup in the basket belonging to Benjamin, the youngest of the group."

Sometime after the brothers set off on their journey, Joseph ordered his steward to gather a party of soldiers to chase after them.

"Tell them that your Lord is angry that they have repaid his kindness with treachery!" instructed Joseph. "Let it be known that the one who has taken my precious silver cup will be severely punished!"

The steward and soldiers made haste on their horses, quickly coming upon the small party of travelers with their donkeys, who were making for Canaan.

When they were confronted with the accusation that Joseph had ordered his steward to present to them, the brothers were astonished.

"Truly, we are not traitors or thieves!" they protested. "Search each one of us, and if any bears your master's cup, then his life will be in your hands, and we remaining will become slaves in your kingdom!"

"So it will be!" snarled the steward, then ordering each of the baskets that the men were carrying to be searched–starting with those of the elder brothers first, and then finally reaching the basket that belonged to Benjamin.

When the cup was pulled out from Benjamin's basket, both he and his brothers were speechless, tearing at their clothes, and unable to control themselves. After much weeping and beating their breasts, they allowed themselves to be led back to the palace, where Joseph awaited them.

When they came before Joseph, Judah spoke on behalf of his family.

"My mighty Lord, I cannot explain how this has happened. Yet more silver has been found in our baskets, and besides, your precious cup was discovered in the basket of our youngest brother! We are now your slaves, for you have found us with these, your possessions!"

Joseph pretended to be angry, but he was restrained in his response.

"Those of you who have only silver coins may return to your father," he commanded. "The young boy will become my slave, for he was the one found to be hiding my silver cup."

Hearing this, Judah prostrated himself before Joseph, begging him that he might make him his slave in place of Benjamin.

"If we return home without our brother Benjamin," Judah pleaded, "Our father will surely die, for he loves his youngest son dearly. He could not bear to see him leave, but we persuaded him that we must bring him, as you had ordered us. Please, Great Lord, consider our father, who is now very old and will not be able to bear this news!"

Joseph was then unable to keep himself from testing his brothers any more. He ordered that all except his kin leave his presence, and then he burst into tears.

"I am your brother! I am Joseph!" he announced. "I am the very one that you threw into the pit, then sold as a slave. How I have longed to make myself known to you! How I yearn to see my father!"

Joseph wailed so loudly, that his cries could be heard throughout the palace. His brothers were astonished, yet were still afraid that he would punish them for their wicked deed.

"Do not be afraid for what you have done!" assured Joseph. "What happened was within God's plan. My coming to Egypt and being brought to a place where I can ensure that both Egypt's people and my own family can be fed are by God's design! Now you must go quickly to fetch my father, for there are many years of famine still to come, and there is good land that you may settle here in Egypt. Now that I am overseer over all, second in command only to Pharaoh himself, your safety here is assured!"

Pharaoh soon heard that Joseph's brothers had come to him, and he repeated Joseph's assurance to them, that they would have all the food that they need, and be well provided for in their new homes. He ordered that many carts be loaded with grain and gifts, then made ready for them to take on their long journey home to their father, beseeching them to return soon with the old man traveling at their side.

With new clothes, and gifts of silver, the men set off back to Canaan.

When they came to their father, the brothers told him all that had happened, showing him the many gifts and bountiful grain that had been sent back on the carts, and presenting Pharaoh's and Joseph's wish that he accompany them to a place where this family, a family called Israel, could settle in a place of safety and abundance.

Jacob could scarcely believe his eyes at the sight of the many gifts. While he was sad to leave his homeland, he trusted God that his son Joseph was still alive, and seeing the gifts that had been sent to him, resolved to see his beloved son one more time.

Jacob then came with his sons, and all their families, journeying many miles across the desert to settle in what would be their new home. This God had promised was right for him to do. Even many miles before coming to Joseph's palace, Jacob saw Joseph in his chariot riding toward him.

When Joseph stepped down from his chariot and Jacob from his cart, the two men stood, staring unbelievingly and lovingly at each other for a short moment. Then Joseph rushed toward his father, and seized him in a firm embrace.

"You have come, my dear father, you have come!" cried Joseph. "All will be provided for you here. The best land is waiting for you, and I myself will arrange for you to meet Pharaoh. Tell him that you are shepherds, and that you have brought your flocks with you. He will surely welcome you, and grant you everything you need!"

When a number of brothers were presented to Pharaoh and he asked them what was their profession, they told him that they were shepherds. Then Pharaoh granted them land as Joseph had predicted, even letting those with special skills be put in charge of his own livestock.

Jacob also came before Pharaoh, and blessed him. With his family, he then settled in the region of Rameses, as Pharaoh had ordained.

The famine continued for five more years. The people of Egypt came to Joseph, begging for food. He took possession of their land for Pharaoh in exchange for grain, and then provided seeds for them to plant, but on condition that one fifth of what they harvested should be returned to Pharaoh.

And so, through Joseph's wise actions, Pharaoh inherited all the land of Egypt, and came to receive a portion of each harvest to add to his own store.

Jacob and his family led happy and prosperous lives. The old man lived a full seventeen years more before he died, and saw many grandchildren and great grandchildren born.

Before he died, Jacob blessed each of his sons, and made an agreement with his beloved son Joseph that his body should be returned to be buried in Canaan once he departed from this world. Joseph obeyed his father's wishes when the time came, carrying him back to his homeland, accompanied by a large entourage of his family and high-ranking Egyptians.

Joseph fully forgave his brothers for what they had done to him, as his heavenly Father had insisted that he do. He reminded them that it was God's Will that had led to him first being taken to Egypt, and that the family would survive, indeed being the first in the line of the great nation of Israel.

Joseph also lived to a great age, seeing both his grandchildren and great grandchildren born. When he died, the people mourned his passing for many weeks and months. His body rested in a coffin for many years, until he too was finally buried in Canaan, the land where he was born.

So ends the story of Joseph, who, with God's help, was saved from dying in a stinking hole to become one of the most powerful and famous men in the world!

CHAPTER FIVE

The Story of Moses and The Great Exodus

A VERY LONG TIME AGO lived a people who were known as the Israelites, who were much loved by God. The Israelites lived in a land called Egypt, which was then ruled over by a very powerful man known as Pharaoh. They worked hard, and were made to do anything that Pharaoh wanted. Yet after many years in Egypt, this much weatherworn people longed to leave the country, to venture to the place where their ancestors had once lived, and which they still thought of as their real home.

More and more, the Israelites became unhappy with the demands that Pharaoh put upon them. As their numbers increased, Pharaoh too became worried that this unhappy people might start to cause trouble. So, he hatched a plan to kill every one of their newborn sons.

"With fewer boys being born," thought the evil Pharaoh, "It will be much harder for the Israelites to fight me, or cause me any trouble!"

Now at this time, a young boy had just been born to an Israelite woman called Jochebed. Knowing that her new baby's life would be in danger were she to bring him up herself, with a very heavy heart, Jochebed wrapped her child in a blanket, placing him in a basket to float on the water among the bulrushes of the mighty River Nile.

"Perhaps my dear child will be found by someone who can bring him up as her own," cried Jochebed. "I do not know what more I can do, for if my baby stays with me, he will surely not survive!"

And so it was that this tiny child was left alone in a basket, rocking gently in the wind by the riverbank, while his poor mother did not know whether he would live or die.

Jochebed had an elder daughter, who stood watching by the riverbank, wondering what might become of her beloved baby brother. Soon, the daughter of Pharaoh came by with her entourage, seeking to bathe in the river. She at once noticed the basket, and commanded one of her maidservants to bring it to her. When she saw that there was a young baby resting inside, she was filled with pity.

Jochebed's daughter then approached the princess and asked whether she might fetch one of the Israelite women, who might nurse the baby on her behalf.

The princess agreed to this plan, and so the woman rushed to her mother and led her to the royal party, where she might be reunited with her baby. The princess took the child into the palace to live with her as her own son, bringing Jochebed too, entrusting her to nurse the young boy. She gave him the name Moses, which means "one who was drawn out from the water."

When he was older, Moses dressed like an Egyptian, and his own people, the Israelites, did not know who he really was. Moses watched his kinsfolk work hard in the fields, while Pharaoh became rich because of their labor.

This grieved Moses very much. One day, when he saw an Egyptian beating an Israelite because he was not working hard enough, Moses's rage became so great that he came out from his hiding place and killed the wicked slave driver. Moses thought that what he did hadn't been seen by anyone, but later when Moses tried to stop an argument among two of the Israelites, one of those who was arguing told him that his crime was no secret.

"Who are you to be a judge of what is right and wrong?" growled the man angrily. "I know that you killed an Egyptian, and so should not tell others what they may do!"

Fearing what might happen to him were Pharaoh to learn that he had killed an Egyptian, Moses ran away to a distant land. There, he came upon a well, where a group of shepherds were frightening several young women, who had come to the well to fetch water for their father's sheep.

Moses saw what was happening, and feeling angry that the women were being treated so poorly, stood up to challenge the men, making sure that the women were able to fill their buckets with water, then return to their father.

The women were amazed by Moses's bravery, and told their father that he had saved them from being attacked. Their old father beckoned his daughters to bring Moses to him, such that he could repay his kindness. And so it was that Moses came to stay with this family, and in time married one of the daughters, whose name was Zipporah.

After some years, Pharaoh died, and a new king came to rule in Egypt. This Pharaoh was no kinder than the other toward the Israelites, and he insisted that they continue to work hard, allowing them no time to have free for themselves.

Day after day, the Israelites labored under the hot sun in the fields, and building houses, and palaces, and huge monuments for Pharaoh. Many were treated very badly by their masters. They hated their lot, yearning to leave Egypt, so that they could return to the homeland of their ancestors. But Pharaoh refused to let them leave.

"If I agree to the Israelites' demand," said Pharaoh, "Who will work the farms and build the buildings where we Egyptians must live?"

Still, God Himself had made a promise with the Israelites, who were a people that He loved like a mother or father loves their children. God had promised that the Israelites would not always be slaves, and that a time would come when He would lead them back to the land of their ancestors. This was a land where many plants grew, and the farms produced rich and delicious foods. This was a place that they could call their own home, and where they could build a great nation.

"It is time," thought God. "My children have suffered for long enough, and I see that this new Pharaoh's heart is not melting. Now, I will make Myself known, and bring the children of My great servants Abraham, Isaac, and Jacob into freedom!"

God saw Moses looking after the sheep of his father-in-law, and knew that he had a good sense of what was right and what was wrong. So, one day, God caused a bush to set alight, close by where Moses was wandering. However, God did not allow the bush to be burned to cinders by the flames.

Moses saw this strange sight, and came close to marvel at it. Then God spoke to him, "Take off your sandals, for you are treading on holy ground!"

Moses did as God commanded, and bowed down some distance away from the bush, which continued to amaze him!

"You are to go to Pharaoh," said God, "And tell him that I have spoken. You are to ask him to allow My people, the Israelites, time to go into the wilderness for three days, where they might worship Me.

"Pharaoh will not allow you to leave your homes, for he is a jealous man. Join with the elders of your kin and tell them what I have told you. I promise to lead you to safety, and will reveal many wonderful signs to show that I am on your side!"

Trembling, Moses bowed lower, unsure why God had chosen him to carry out such a perilous task.

"Who am I, a humble shepherd, to make this request to Pharaoh?" cried Moses. "What will my life be worth if Pharaoh doesn't believe me?"

God then told Moses to throw his stick onto the ground.

In an instant, the stick turned into a large snake, terrifying Moses.

"Grab the tail of the snake by your hand!" commanded God.

While he was very afraid, Moses did as God had told him, and the snake immediately changed back into the stick that he had been carrying in his hand!

"Now put your hand inside your coat, then take it out again," commanded God.

Moses did as he was told, and saw that his skin was immediately covered in terrible spots and blisters.

"Now put your hand in your coat one more time, and then bring it out again!" said God.

Moses followed God's command, and was immediately healed of his unsightly condition.

"Perhaps some people may fear the signs, but Pharaoh will be very hard to persuade!" warned God.

"If you perform these signs, and he does not believe that I have spoken to you," said God, "Then take some water and pour it onto the ground. This will make the waters of The Nile turn into blood!"

Moses trusted that what God said would come to be, but he believed that he was unsuitable to speak on God's behalf.

"I am not good with words," said Moses. "Surely there is a person more able than I who can speak to pharaoh?"

"O my feeble son!" replied God, angrily. "Who apart from I gives you a mouth with which to speak? Who other than I makes you wise?"

God saw that Moses was afraid, and so He agreed that his elder brother, Aaron, might accompany him and be his mouthpiece. "Still it will be you who instructs Aaron what to say," said God. "And it is you who has seen these signs, in order that you might show them to others, so that they too might believe!"

God spoke to Aaron, and Moses told his brother all that God had instructed him to do. Together, they gathered the elders of the Israelites, then told them what God had said, revealing to them the signs that God had shown to Moses. The elders trusted that God had spoken to Moses and his brother, and gave them their blessing to petition Pharaoh on their behalf.

Moses and Aaron then sought an audience with Pharaoh, trusting that it was God's will that they should do so.

"Mighty Pharaoh, allow our people just three days to worship our God alone in the wilderness!" pleaded the brothers. "This is what God has told us we must do, and no man can deny His Will!"

Pharaoh was impressed by the bravery of Moses and Aaron, but his heart was hard, and he saw that if he let the Israelites go, no work would be done in the fields and about his palace for three whole days!

"Your God is not my God!" replied Pharaoh. "I will not let you go, for you are slaves to Egypt and to me. Now go quickly from my presence, before my anger turns against you!"

Moses and Aaron came away from the palace, wondering what they might do next.

Pharaoh became very angry at the boldness of their request, and commanded the slave drivers who oversaw the work of the Israelites to make their work even harder.

"They must now find their own straw to make bricks with!" he demanded, "Do not give them what they need for their work, nor cut down the number of bricks that they must bring to you each day. Now, we will see if they make any more outrageous demands!"

The slave drivers showed no mercy in following Pharaoh's command. They made the Israelites work harder and harder, beating anyone who did not bring them what they demanded.

Soon, the Israelites became angry with Moses and Aaron because of the extra work that was expected of them.

"You with your foolish request!" they cried. "It is because of you that we now suffer more than ever before!"

Moses and his brother were very troubled by the Israelites' anger, and so they came to a quiet place where they might ask God what they should do next.

"I Am God!" said God. "I always honor My promise. So will Pharaoh allow you to leave this land, but only after both you and he have been much tested!

"Go to the tyrant king, and ask again that My people be set free to worship Me!" commanded God.

"Let Pharaoh see the signs that I have shown to you, and many more besides. Do not lose heart, because I will always be with you!"

Moses and Aaron bowed down before God, and promised to do as He had commanded, while they were afraid. The brothers traveled again to meet Pharaoh, and begged him to allow the Israelites their freedom. But Pharaoh again refused.

Moses then showed Pharaoh the first of the signs that God had revealed to him beside the burning bush. He threw his stick onto the bright cobblestones of Pharaoh's palace, and immediately the stick turned into an enormous snake!

Pharaoh was alarmed, and quickly beckoned his closest advisors and sorcerers to come to him, to see if they could make sense of this strange happening.

Some of the sorcerers performed an act with the sticks that they were holding. When they threw these onto the stone ground, these too changed into snakes! But at once, the giant snake that had been formed from Moses's stick ate up all the others.

Pharaoh's heart was unmoved, and he suspected Moses and Aaron of trickery. So he sent them away again, refusing to heed their request.

Moses and Aaron once more consulted with God, Who told them to approach Pharaoh while he was bathing near the River Nile.

"Take your stick and strike the river with it!" God told Moses. "Open wide your arms and put a curse upon the waters!" He told Aaron. "Tell Pharaoh that by these acts, the water will turn to blood, and no one will be able to drink it!"

The following morning, Moses and Aaron did as God commanded.

Still, Pharaoh refused to allow the Israelites to go. Pharaoh again called together his advisors and sorcerers, among whom were those whose secret arts had taught them how to turn water into blood.

One week passed by, and God again spoke to Moses and Aaron, telling them to now warn Pharaoh that He would bring a plague of frogs to the country if Pharaoh continued to keep His people like slaves.

"Tell Pharaoh that the frogs will be so great in number, that no one will be able to escape from them! They will come into his palace and jump all over him, and be everywhere about!"

The following day, Moses and Aaron went to Pharaoh once more, bringing him news of what God had promised. Once again, Pharaoh refused their request, and so God sent the plague of frogs that he had warned about. Pharaoh's sorcerers made frogs appear too, but these were very few in number compared with those that came into the palace upon Moses and Aaron's calling.

The frogs came into Pharaoh's bedchamber, and crowded onto his throne, croaking and spreading a great smell around them as they did so.

Finally, Pharaoh could stand the frogs no more. He ordered Moses and Aaron to be brought before him, demanding that they pray to their God to bring the terrible plague to an end.

"We will offer our prayers at the time of your choosing," they said. "Then you will know that our God listens to our prayers!"

This they then did, and all the frogs disappeared. Yet still, Pharaoh would not change his mind, still not allowing the Israelites their freedom.

God then told Moses and Aaron that He would bring a new plague upon Pharaoh, because he remained stubborn, not being kind to the Israelites.

"Take your stick and strike it upon the ground right in front of Pharaoh!" ordered God. "All of the dust underneath your feet will turn into gnats, which will bite the people, and cause them much agony!"

This Moses and Aaron then did, and great swarms of gnats filled the air. They came into the Egyptians' houses, and filled the rooms of the palace. Soon, people were crying out in pain, for they were being bitten all over.

Pharaoh called together his advisors and sorcerers, but they did not know how to perform a similar deed to what Moses and Aaron had shown them.

"This is surely an act of the true God!" they declared. But still Pharaoh would not listen.

"Now I will bring a plague of flies upon the land!" God then told the brothers. "But the flies will not affect my children, only Pharaoh and the Egyptians!"

Moses and Aaron told Pharaoh what God had planned for them, but Pharaoh continued to ignore their pleas to let them leave.

So it was that the plague of flies terrorized the Egyptians, destroying their crops, and making the people's lives a misery.

When he could stand it no more, Pharaoh summoned Moses and Aaron before him, promising to allow them to lead the Israelites into the wilderness for three days, where they might make their offerings to God.

Moses and Aaron promised to pray for the flies to go away, but warned Pharaoh that he must honor his promise too. But no sooner than the flies had disappeared, than Pharaoh again turned back on his promise.

God then brought another plague upon the land. This time, all the farm animals belonging to Egyptians were killed, though not a single one that was looked after by the Israelites was harmed.

Pharaoh saw that only the animals of the Israelites were spared, but still he would not open his heart and allow the Israelites their freedom.

God then told Moses and Aaron to return to Pharaoh, taking with them handfuls of soot that they had gathered from a furnace.

"When you throw the soot into the air," said God, "I will cause painful blisters and sores to break out on the skin of Pharaoh, his advisors, sorcerers, and all his people. They will be in such pain, that they will not even be able to stand before you!"

Moses and Aaron again went before Pharaoh to present their case and bring God's warning. Yet Pharaoh still would not listen to them. They then threw the soot that they had brought with them into the air, and immediately, Pharaoh, his advisors, sorcerers, and all his people were covered in the most ugly and painful sores. The people scratched and scratched, and cried out in agony, but their pain would not go away!

God saw that Pharaoh would not change his mind. So He called Moses and Aaron to Him, and told them to again confront Pharaoh the following morning. God told them to warn Pharaoh that if the evil tyrant still would not allow Moses and his companions time of their own to worship their God, this time a plague would come that was far worse than any they had seen before!

"Tell this evil tyrant that if he does not have a change of heart, I will bring the fiercest storm that has ever been known in this land! Giant hailstones will rain down from the sky. Thunder and lightning will strike out over the land. Not a single person or animal that is left outside will survive! Tell Pharaoh that I, in My mercy, could have struck him and his army down many times before now, yet I have spared him to reveal the greatness of My power!"

Moses and Aaron faced Pharaoh again, warning him that his refusal to heed their request would bring about this terrible storm. Only those who listened to their warning, trusting the word of the true God, would be spared. All those who did not, and who stayed outside or who left their animals to wander freely in the fields, would be killed.

Yet Pharaoh continued to refuse the Israelites freedom to go away to worship their God. Moses and Aaron then stretched out their arms, and the most terrible storm broke out over Egypt, in every part of the land, except for the place where the Israelites were.

All day and all night, hailstones fell, flooding the ground. Blinding blue lightning cracked open the sky, while thunder boomed louder and louder. Countless trees were torn from their roots, and the hailstones destroyed the first of the harvests. Not a single animal or person that was outside when the storm came was saved. Never before had such a tragedy been known in all of Egypt.

Fearing that the storm would never end, Pharaoh summoned Moses and Aaron and pleaded with them to pray that peace might be brought back to the land.

"I have strayed from God," cried Pharaoh. "I see now that yours is the true God, and that I have been at fault! I promise that if you ask God to end the storm, I will do what is right, and let you have the freedom that you desire!"

Moses and Aaron then left the palace, and pleaded with God to end the storm. The hailstones finally stopped falling, and the clouds became bright again, then revealing the sun, which shone brightly once more upon the land.

Moses and Aaron believed that this time Pharaoh might honor his promise. But no sooner had the storm ended, than he again hardened his heart, commanding once again that the Israelites not be allowed to leave their work.

God again called to His faithful servants, telling them that He was working these many signs so that all future generations could be sure that He is a mighty and faithful God!

"This time, I will send a plague of locusts upon the land!" decreed God. "Many, many in number will they be, all hungry for food. They will settle on every blade of grass, and eat all the food that is left on the trees. They will go into the houses, and storerooms, and all the chambers of the palace. Soon, there will be no food left for Pharaoh or his people to eat!"

So, Moses and Aaron went to Pharaoh, and stretched out their arms to bring the plague of locusts upon the people. As God had forewarned, the locusts devoured everything within their sight, and were to be found everywhere that there were people.

"This is beyond what I can bear!" cried Pharaoh to his advisors. "Bring Moses and Aaron to me again, such that I may ask them to pray for the locusts to leave!"

Pharaoh pleaded with Moses and Aaron to pray for him, claiming that he was truly sorry for again doing wrong. "Forgive this evil man, and I will let all the Israelite men go!" he cried.

Moses and Aaron pleaded with God to take the locusts away from Egypt, and God sent a powerful wind that drove the clouds of large, black insects into the sea. Yet Pharaoh still would not allow the women and children of Israel to go.

Once again, God revealed to Moses and Aaron the terror that would now fall upon Pharaoh, if he continued not to allow the Israelites to leave.

"Now I will bring total darkness upon the land. Not a single person will be able to see any thing, and they will fear for the darkness, which will overwhelm them, and haunt them, and give them no respite from their terror.

"Among the Israelites, My people, I will shine light. They will still be able to see! Go now and tell Pharaoh what I have ordained!"

So Moses and Aaron went again to Pharaoh, who despite their warning, still refused to allow the Israelites to go. The two faithful servants of God then held out their arms, and darkness fell upon the land for many days, blinding all the people. That is, all except God's people, who continued to have light in their homes.

Fearing the end for his kingdom, Pharaoh sent again for Moses and Aaron, pleading with them to pray that God would bring the darkness to an end.

"This time you may all go!" promised Pharaoh. "All your men, women and children may leave this land. But you must leave your livestock here, since these are needed by my people."

Yet Moses and Aaron refused to accept Pharaoh's offer. "We will leave, but with our animals too!" they replied. "For these we need to travel with us."

"Then be gone from my sight forever!" hollered Pharaoh. "If you come near me again, I will surely strike you down!"

Moses and Aaron then left the furious king, never to set eyes upon him again. Yet Pharaoh still hardened his heart, still refusing the Israelites a safe passage to leave his land.

God called upon Moses and Aaron, telling them that He would perform one more sign, which would be the very last one before Pharaoh would allow them to leave.

"This last time, Pharaoh will not hesitate to let you go!" promised God. "You are to call the elders of the Israelites together and tell them that at an appointed hour, every family is to make an offering of a lamb to Me. They must take a little of its blood, which they are to use to put a mark on the doors of their houses. They are to roast the lamb, and eat it, along with herbs.

"After midnight on this very day, I will send My army of angels. They will visit every family in Egypt and strike down the life of every firstborn child. Not a single family will be spared–not the firstborn of Pharaoh himself, nor that of a prisoner who wallows in his dungeons. No firstborn of any of their animals will be saved besides!

"Yet I promise that no one whose house is marked with the sign of lamb's blood will be harmed. My angels will pass over their houses, and there will be no crying among your animals, for they too will be saved.

"For those whose homes are unmarked, there will be terrible suffering. Mothers will cry out for their lost children. Animals will be heard wailing in the fields. All of Egypt will grieve after this terrible night. And Pharaoh will then let My people go!"

Moses and Aaron then gathered the elders of their people together and told them what God had promised. In turn, the elders went among the people, telling them what they must do when the appointed hour came.

And so it was, that the people of Israel sacrificed lambs, as God had commanded them, and marked their houses such that His angels would pass over them on the night that God wrought his vengeance on Egypt.

When he heard the wailing, and saw what was happening, even the death of his own beloved son, Pharaoh joined his people in crying out aloud, and finally demanded that Moses and Aaron lead their people out of his land without further delay.

"Go!" Pharaoh pleaded. "Go now, right away! Take all your animals–just go! Leave us in peace, and pray that your God will have mercy upon us!"

Then finally, Moses and Aaron gathered all of their people together, and began to lead them away from the country where they had lived as slaves for so long. They took all their animals, and also many gifts of gold and silver that the people of Egypt gave to them, for God had melted their hearts in favor of His people.

In their hundreds of thousands they gathered, ready to begin a long journey to their homeland that became known as "The Great Exodus."

The people left so quickly, that they didn't have time to use yeast to make their bread. Moses reminded the people that God had for long promised that He would free them from slavery, and bring them to their homeland. So it was that they celebrated this special day, and it continues to be remembered until our own time.

The journey to the land of the Israelites' ancestors was a long one, involving many dangers and a crossing over a vast desert. God knew that His people would face many dangers taking the shortest route, so He led them first towards the wide expanse of the Red Sea. So that they knew where to go, God sent a great cloud ahead of the people to show them the way. At nighttime, He sent a tower of fire to guide their path and lead them ever forward.

It was not long before Pharaoh realized how great was his loss for allowing the Israelites to flee. All the hard work that the Israelites had done now had to be carried out by other slaves, or by the Egyptians themselves. Quickly regretting his decision, Pharaoh decided that he would assemble his large army, to go after the Israelites before they had traveled very far.

He amassed six hundred armour-plated chariots, along with many more. With his generals, and his soldiers, and all his horses, he quickly came to where he could see where the Israelites were camping. The Israelites were terrified when they saw Pharaoh's fearsome army approaching, believing that they might soon be surrounded and be crushed under foot.

"Now we will perish by the sword, when it would have been better for us to die as the slaves of our old masters!" they cried out. "You, Moses and Aaron, have brought us to our graves. It is because of you that we are now here!"

Moses and Aaron still trusted God, and promised the people that He would continue to guide them.

"We must have faith and be strong!" pleaded Moses. "God is on our side, as He has always been. He will save us!"

Moses cried out to God, Who told him to stretch out his arms, as though ordering the sea to make a passage for him. As Moses did as God commanded him, the sea that was close by where the Israelites were camping opened up to reveal a long strip of land that had until then been at the seabed, over which Moses, his brother, and all the Israelites could flee.

God sent a great cloud to stand between the Israelites and Pharaoh's army, and a pillar of fire by night to light their way across to the other side of the sea.

As darkness fell, the Israelites crossed the mighty Red Sea, as though they were passing over dry land. One by one, they reached the other side, until all were gathered safely on the far bank.

Now the Egyptians had found the place of their crossing, and attempted to charge their horses towards them. But the heavy wheels of their chariots soon became clogged in the mud, and in the darkness, great confusion grew among Pharaoh's army.

When he saw that all the Israelites had crossed from the far bank of the sea, Moses held out his arms once more, then drew them together. At once, the powerful waves of the sea returned to the place where the Israelites had made their crossing, quickly filling the space that had once been there. All of the Egyptians who were stuck, and the horses, and the foot soldiers who were following them behind were drowned in the deep, dark water.

When the Israelites saw what God had done, they were filled with great wonder and love for Him. They sung aloud, and worshipped the One Whom they now knew to be a God Who always keeps His promises!

God promised to lead His people ever nearer to their home, but soon they were doubting Him once more. To green oases He led them when they were thirsty for water, and fine food known as manna He brought for them from the sky when they were hungry. God brought the Israelites to victory in battle and led them far away from Egypt, yet still they began to turn against Him.

Moses remained faithful to his God. And so it was Moses that God called to meet with Him alone on top of a mountain known as Mount Sinai, where God told him the way by which He wanted His people to live. These instructions became known as "The Ten Commandments," telling us that we must not steal, or kill, or be jealous; we must not make false gods or worship anything or anyone other than the one true God; we must not tell lies, hurt those whom we love, or want for things that our neighbors have. We should please our father and mother, and be kind to each other.

God inscribed these commandments on two large stone tablets, which Moses took with him when he finally came down from the mountain.

However, Moses had been away for forty days listening to God. In the meantime, the Israelites had become impatient and persuaded Aaron that they needed something that they could idolize and make offerings to. So they had melted down the golden rings and pots and plates that they had brought with them from Egypt, to make a large statue of a calf.

When Moses approached the Israelites' camp after his long time away, he saw what they had done, and cried out at their foolishness and lack of faith.

"Oh you wicked people!" he cried. "I have been away for just a short time, yet so quickly you have turned your hearts away from God!"

So sad was Moses when he saw the golden calf that the people had made, that he threw the stone tablets that God had given him onto the ground, breaking them into pieces. Yet soon, he made a new pair of tablets, and wrote upon them the instructions that God had given to him.

Moses demanded that those who had disobeyed God and worshipped the golden calf be severely punished. He then set the people to work, making sure they obeyed all that God had told him they should do.

This included building a beautiful place where the Israelites could worship God, and a precious cabinet, made of gold and fine acacia wood, to house the tablets bearing God's laws, which was known as the "Ark Of The Covenant."

God instructed His servants to ordain priests. He described the clothes they were to wear, and the rituals they were to perform. He made known the rules by which the people should live by, such that there might not be arguments and fighting among them.

God then led the people to a place where they might set sight upon some of the land that He planned for their inheritance.

Moses instructed scouts to go out into the land to inspect it, and then to report back to him about what they discovered.

When they completed their mission, the scouts confirmed that the land was very rich and green, making it a very welcoming place to settle. Yet they also reported that the people who lived there were giants, who would surely crush the Israelites, were they to go into battle against them.

"We have seen them with our own eyes," the scouts announced. "No one among us will be able to fight them, for these people are much stronger than us!"

As they had before, the Israelites cried out to Moses and Aaron.

"You have brought us to this place, which we have no hope of making a home!" they cried. "How wretched are we! It would be better had we never left Egypt. There, we at least had promise of shelter and food to eat!"

Moses and Aaron trusted that God would continue to look after His people, even though the situation seemed to be very bleak. God promised that this would be so, but because the people had doubted Him, He decreed that only their young and the faithful would finally reach what we now know as "the promised land."

So it was that the Israelites wandered in the desert for a further forty years before their next generation was fully grown and ready at last to enter the land that God had made ready for them.

Moses was now very old, and knew that he would die before long. With the many families of Israel surrounding him, Moses gave them his last blessing and sang a song of praise to the God Who had never abandoned him. Then he went to the top of a mountain from where he could see the beautiful green valleys of the land that God had promised for his offspring, and there gave up his spirit to be always with the God Who he so loved. And God looks after him still, as He does all who love Him.

CHAPTER SIX
Joshua, God's Warrior

FOLLOWING THE DEATH OF MOSES, the great leader of the Israelites, God commanded his servant Joshua to continue his ancestor's work.

Before God guided Moses and his brother Aaron to lead the Israelites into freedom, they had been slaves in Egypt for many hundreds of years. Many disobeyed God, and so even after escaping Pharaoh's power, they had continued to roam in the wilderness for an entire generation.

Now they had sighted what was to be their new homeland, a land that God had promised to set aside for them. God then called Joshua, and told him to make ready to cross over the River Jordan, and lead His people into a place that was said to flow with milk and honey.

"The time is now right, My son," said God, "For My promise to be fulfilled.

"Under My protection, within three days, you, and all of the children of Israel, shall cross the River Jordan, and set foot in the land that I have set aside for you!

"Rich and vast lands await you, stretching from the Euphrates River in the east to the shores of the Mediterranean Sea in the west. In this land you will find deserts, mountains, and fertile plains. There too, you will seize cities and villages from the evil kings that now inhabit there.

"Many battles lie ahead that you will need to fight. But do not be afraid, for I will always be with you and give you victory! Have courage, and be strong. Honor Me, and follow My Word. Do this, and you will never lack for anything that you need!"

Joshua bowed low before God, his heart overflowing with gratitude. He then returned to speak with the elders of his people, and afterward addressed the whole nation.

"For many years, we have wandered in the desert. Finally, God has brought us to this place where we can see the land that He has set aside for us. Within three days, we will cross the River Jordan, and claim this land as our own!

"Many battles await us, but God has promised to subdue the many tyrants that we face. We are to keep His

Word, just as our father Moses commanded us to. Let us go forward, being strong and full of courage!"

So it was, amid much excitement, that the Israelites prepared to finally cross into the land that had for so long been promised to them. Within three days, they knew that God's promise would be fulfilled.

Before they came to the River Jordan, Joshua had decided to send two men into the land that lay ahead of them, in order that they might spy on the people there. He ordered them to journey to the city of Jericho, to discern what the people had heard about the Israelites, and the victories that God had won for them.

So the two men set off as Joshua had instructed, coming to the house of a woman in the heavily protected city. She took them in, welcomed them, and promised them food and rest.

"We have heard many things about you Israelites," said the woman. "God surely cares for your people! He led you to freedom from Egypt, even causing the Red Sea to hold back its waters, such that you might cross to safety. In the wilderness, He provided for you, and made you victorious over your enemies. Now we fear that your army is approaching us, and our hearts tremble because of this."

The men were grateful for the woman's testimony, and accepted her humble hospitality.

She then proposed to hide the men from the king's soldiers, since news had reached the palace that there were spies at large within the city. Taking them to the roof of her house, which was set into the city wall, she urged the men to conceal themselves beneath a pile of flax stalks. She then returned to her living quarters to await the visit from the king's guard that she soon expected.

When the soldiers arrived, they asked the woman whether she had spoken with two men, who were thought to be spies.

"Why, yes! I did indeed see two men," the woman replied. "Yet they are now gone from our city. They departed at dusk, just before the city gate was closing. I do not know where they may now be!"

The soldiers then hurried from the woman's house, and set off from the city in pursuit of the fugitives.

When she saw that they were out of sight, the woman then hurried back to her roof to consult with Joshua's men, who were still hiding beneath the pile of flax stalks.

"Soldiers came, enquiring about your whereabouts," she explained to them. "I told them that I had seen you, but that you had left the city. They have now gone in search of you, and I doubt that they will return for several more days.

"My dear friends, I beg that you will honor me with a favor," continued the woman. "Just as I have helped you by protecting you here, I beseech that you spare my life, and the lives of my family also, when you return to take our city."

"This we promise to do," replied the men. "You have shown great kindness to us, and we know that you have acted in the interest of our people, and that you honor our God too.

"However, we may only guarantee your safety, and that of your family also, if you remain in this house when our army arrives. Hang this scarlet cord from your window, so we will know not to enter your house."

The men then handed the woman a length of scarlet cord, which she promptly tied to a metal bar that was set by the side of her window. She then fetched a rope, to allow the men to lower themselves from the window, by which means they could escape outside the city walls.

The men then fled to hide in the hills, where the woman had assured them that the soldiers would not look for them. Following several days, they returned across the River Jordan to give their report to Joshua.

"The city of Jericho is ours to be taken!" they declared. "The people there are afraid of our coming. God is surely on our side!"

The Israelites made camp to the east of the river, excitedly awaiting Joshua's command to pack up their belongings, and cross over with him into what we now know as "the promised land." Yet they did not know how they would be able to cross the fast-flowing river with all their possessions and many animals, fearing that its waters were deep, and its current very strong.

God then spoke to Joshua, telling him what the people should do.

"Now it is time to cross the river," instructed God. "Order the priests who bear My Ark of the Covenant to go ahead of the party, walking straight out into the river. As soon as their feet touch the water, I will cause the river to stop flowing, so that you may cross safely to the other side."

The Ark of the Covenant was a very sacred box, containing two stone tablets upon which was written The Law of God. Only a few selected priests were allowed to carry it, while the rest of the people followed some considerable distance behind.

Joshua related to the people what God had told him, telling them to follow behind the priests. He then instructed the priests to carry the Ark of the Covenant, and to enter into the river's water.

No sooner had the priests' feet touched the water, than the river stopped flowing. God had caused water upstream to be held back by a dam, and within very little time, the place where the Israelites stood became completely dry!

Joshua, and the whole nation of Israel, were then able to cross safely to the other side, while the priests continued to stand on the river bed, faithfully holding the precious Ark of the Covenant.

No less than forty thousand people crossed the river that day, many armed and ready to do battle.

God then commanded Joshua to appoint twelve men from among the tribes of Israel to fetch twelve stones from the middle of the river. These were to be taken to the place where the Israelites made camp that evening, where the stones would serve as a permanent reminder of the miracle that God had performed.

When all had crossed to the west side of the river, the priests followed on behind them.

Once the priests were safely on the far shore, the waters of the river began to flow very quickly once more. Just as He had done for His children when He separated the waters of the Red Sea, so God allowed safe passage across the River Jordan for His people to enter into the promised land.

When the kings of the people who were living west of the Jordan heard what had happened, they were greatly afraid.

"Surely, God is with this people!" they moaned. "Soon, their army will be upon us, and their God will deliver victory into their hands!"

The people of Israel then proceeded to march toward the city of Jericho. As they did so, a commanding man with a sword appeared and stood before them.

"Who are you?" questioned Joshua, when the two men came face-to-face. "Do you come in the name of our enemy, or are you faithful to our side?"

"Neither!" replied the man. "I come as a messenger of God, to go before you. Take off your sandals, for you are standing on holy ground!"

Joshua then did as the messenger commanded, and bowed low before him.

Knowing that Joshua's army was approaching, the people of Jericho were very afraid. The king ordered that the city gates be secured shut. No one was allowed to leave or enter the city. The people stayed in their homes, wondering how long they might survive, for they had little food to feed their animals, and sparse supplies of grain to feed themselves.

God told Joshua what he must do in order to take hold of the city.

"Appoint seven priests," commanded God. "Tell them to make trumpets from rams' horns. These men are to proceed in front of the Ark of the Covenant, sounding their trumpets.

"Appoint a body of men to guard the priests–some marching before the Ark, and some behind.

"Order the guards, and the priests with their trumpets, and the holy men who are responsible for carrying the Ark of the Covenant to circle round outside of the city walls, sounding their trumpets. Do this once on the first day, then continue to make a circuit for each of the following five days. Make no battle cry during this time, no sound other than the call of the trumpets!

"On the seventh day, proceed around the city a full seven times. Then the trumpeters are to sound one loud blast, whereupon the whole army may shout aloud its cry. Then you will see the ancient walls of Jericho fall!"

Joshua repeated what The LORD had told him to the priests and the army. He appointed seven priests to make trumpets from rams' horns, and ordered that no one should make a battle cry until they heard one long blast of the trumpets.

"When the walls crumble," instructed Joshua, "Advance quickly into the city. Kill every woman, man, and child. Take your swords to their animals, and seize the treasures that are considered holy to their king. Yet take none of this for yourselves, for this will bring disrepute upon our people. These are treasures that are intended to honor God, and so must be bought into His temple."

When they were ready, the guards and priests circled the city walls for the first time, just as God and Joshua had commanded. The trumpets sounded as they marched, but not a shout was heard from among the party.

Inside the city, the people heard the trumpets sounding, and were filled with fear. They huddled together in their cellars and under tables, praying that their god might spare their lives.

On the second day, Joshua's men again circled the city. A third day, they did the same. And then on the fourth, and on the fifth, and on the sixth.

On the seventh day, they circled the city a full seven times, still sounding their trumpets. When they had completed their seventh tour around the city, the trumpeters let out a long and very loud blast. This was the signal for all the Israelites to make their battle cry!

Their roar cracked open the sky. As God had promised, when they made their cry, the walls of the once celebrated city came crashing to the ground.

Immediately, the Israelite army stormed into the city. They entered every house, and searched every room, killing every person and every animal that they found. Only the house that hung the scarlet cord from its window was spared. The woman who lived there, the one who had protected Joshua's spies, was taken safely to the Israelites' camp, along with her whole family.

Gold and silver from the Royal Treasury were plundered, and brought back to be kept safe in the temple of the Israelites. When Joshua's army had finished their rampage, and all who lived in Jericho lay dying, the Israelites reassembled at their camp. There, Joshua gave an order to put the city to the torch.

The flames grew quickly, turning the sky blood red, and licking up every body and every brick that stood in their way. Soon, only a small pile of rubble remained where the once impenetrable city had stood.

Jericho's fate became known far and wide, and many kings and their people feared the might of the Israelites. They feared that Joshua's army would soon come looking for them, and their fate would be the same as that that had befallen Jericho.

Following their victory, Joshua sent spies to inspect the city of Ai, which was his next target for attack. The spies completed their mission, reporting back to him that the city would be easy to take, not requiring more than a small company of soldiers.

Heeding their advice, Joshua then allowed most of his army to rest, sending only a small number to lay siege on Ai.

Yet this time, the Israelites found no easy victory. All the people of Ai took up arms, surprising the Israelites with their might, chasing them from the city, and even killing a few.

When he heard what had happened, Joshua felt despair. Prostrating himself before God, he cried out, fearing that further campaigns would lead to the Israelites' destruction.

"Why, My LORD, have you allowed this to happen?" cried Joshua. "When the other kings see how easily we were defeated at Ai, they will surely amass their armies against us, and we will be crushed by them!"

"Where is your faith, My son?" answered God. "Have I not promised you that the land that lies before you will be yours?

"Be strong, and have courage! You were defeated at Ai because there is one among you who has disobeyed Me, taking treasure that was intended for My temple into their own tent. When Israel is disobedient, you forsake My protection. Yet when you are for Me, I will always ensure your victory!

"Go, and command all the tribes of Israel to gather together. I will direct you to one from the twelve tribes that is to come forward. From this tribe, I will instruct you which clan holds the one who has stolen from Me. From this clan, you will learn the family, and then the thief himself will be identified. Search them, and if they are found guilty, they, their family, livestock, and all of their possessions must be destroyed!"

Just as God commanded, Joshua ordered all the tribes of Israel to come together. God then directed which of the twelve tribes Joshua should call forward. He then identified the clan that the evil person belonged to. Then the family was named, and finally the individual himself, whose name was Achan.

Achan told Joshua what he had done. His tent was then searched, and buried there were found gold, silver, and a precious robe.

"I have been unfaithful to my people, and to my God," Achan confessed. "I wanted these things for myself, as they appeared beautiful to me. I know that I have stolen from God Himself, and for this, there can be no mercy."

Joshua then ordered that Achan, his family, his animals, and all his possessions be destroyed. The treasures that Achan had stolen were gathered together, and brought into the LORD's temple.

God then told Joshua to take his whole army and return to Ai once more. "Do not be afraid," promised God. "This time, I will ensure your victory!"

Guided by God, Joshua divided his troops. One small group he took with himself, while the remainder he commanded to remain in hiding close to Ai, but outside the walls of the city, such that they might set upon the army of Ai when it came chasing after Joshua and his small party.

Joshua then led his men toward the city, just as the small group of soldiers had before. Seeing this tiny band, the people of Ai were certain that they could quickly overcome them, as they had before. The king of Ai did not hesitate in ordering his army to attack Joshua and his men, chasing them far away from the city walls.

Yet they did not know that an ambush was waiting for them. At a chosen moment, Joshua held out his javelin, as God had commanded him to, and the many thousands of Israelites who were waiting in hiding set upon the army of Ai, quickly subduing them.

Joshua then returned to his camp, where he instructed an altar to be built to honor God. This faithful servant of The LORD reminded the people what God had done for them, and the way that He wanted them to live.

When they heard about Joshua's victory at Ai, and remembered the destruction of Jericho, the kings of the lands that had been promised to the Israelites gathered together to decide what they should do. If they fought together, some reasoned, they might present a formidable force to the Israelites, driving them back across to the east of the Jordan River.

Yet one group of people whose lives were threatened by Joshua's army invented a story by which to deceive the Israelites. By doing this, they hoped to save their skins.

This people, the Gibeonites, loaded donkeys with battered and worn saddlebags, which they filled with moldy bread. They tore at their clothes, and dirtied their faces, as if to appear as though they had been traveling for many miles.

They then came to the Israelites, claiming that they wanted to make a peace treaty with them.

"We are from a distant land," began the Gibeonites. "We have heard about your famous victories, and know that your God has performed many mighty deeds. We come to seek peace with you!"

The Israelites who received the delegation did not consult with God, but were convinced by the men's appearance, the state of their saddlebags, and the smell of their moldy bread, that they had traveled from a distant land.

They then vowed to live in peace with the travelers, but soon learned that they had been deceived.

"Why have you lied to us?" demanded the Israelites, when they learned of the deception. "You are neighbors, living on land that has been promised to us, yet you claim that you have traveled from far away!"

"We were afraid for our lives," replied the Gibeonites." Please show mercy upon us. We are now your servants!"

Remembering their solemn vow to live in peace, the Israelites agreed to spare the lives of the Gibeonites. Yet Joshua warned them that they would always be slaves to Israel, becoming woodcutters and water bearers in Israel's service.

Some of the other kings then became vengeful towards the Gibeonites. Rulers from five kingdoms came together, resolving to invade the Gibeonites' land, and then put them to the sword.

The Gibeonites begged Joshua to defend them, and this he promised to do. The Israelites chased the invaders from the Gibeonites' land, slaying many thousands, including the five kings.

As He had always done before, God prepared the way for the Israelites' course to victory. He sent giant hailstones to fall upon the fleeing enemy, and even permitted the sun and moon to stand still in the sky at Joshua's command. Never before, and never since, has such a sight been seen!

When they were captured, the bodies of the kings were hanged on tall poles, where vultures picked at their flesh. They were then thrown into a cave, which was sealed with a giant boulder, never again to be opened.

God led the Israelites to many more famous battles. Kingdoms to the north, south, and west were conquered, adding to the lands that had already been claimed to the east. Joshua then began the task of dividing the land that was now the Israelites' home among the twelve tribes.

Some of the people returned east of the Jordan river, to land that had earlier been designated for them by Moses. There, they built an altar just like the altar of The LORD that stood on the west bank of the river, such that they may never forget who is the true LORD.

Joshua was now very old, and he knew that it would soon be time for him to join his LORD in heaven. He therefore called together representatives from all of the tribes of Israel, to bid them goodbye, and to remind them once more of God's great promise.

"You have seen with your own eyes what God has done for us," stated Joshua. "He has kept all of His promises. Not once has He failed us. So we too must always be faithful to Him. Let none among us ever turn away from serving God. We may be sure that if we do, He will no longer defend us. Always be faithful, always be strong. Take courage, and go forward to enjoy all that He delights in giving!"

The people bowed down before Joshua one last time, promising to always honor God.

Joshua then passed on, to always be with his God, having fought many battles, and always staying faithful to his LORD.

So ends our story of Joshua, the strong and courageous warrior for God.

CHAPTER SEVEN

Samson, The Strong

IN THE LAND OF ANCIENT ISRAEL, there once was a time when no kings or queens ruled. At this time, God's people suffered many hardships, often being brought into poverty after fighting with their neighbors. Time and again, they needed to hear clearly from God, to know what was His purpose for them.

To lead the people through these times of difficulty, God appointed brave men and women to come forward and make His purpose known. He gave them wisdom, and many gifts that they would need to make their voices heard, and to be successful in facing the many dangers that lay ahead of them.

These brave people were known as "judges". Among them was a man named Samson, who had been born to a family from the land of Zorah. Samson came as a special gift for his mother, who had been unable to bear children. She had cried out in her desperation to have a child, pleading with God that He might allow her to fall pregnant.

Grieving for her plight, God sent an angel to speak to her.

"Do not be afraid, dear child!" assured the angel. "You will soon give birth to a son, who will become great in this nation!

"Your son is to make a vow to God that he will never take drinks that might lead him to drunkenness, nor use a razor to cut his hair!"

Believing that what the angel had said would come to be, the woman was overjoyed, and rushed to tell her husband, whose name was Manoah.

Manoah begged his wife to call upon God again, in order that they might know how they should raise their child when he was born.

God's angel returned to his wife, and she called out to her husband to come to see the miraculous apparition that was in front of her.

When he approached the angel, Manoah asked how he should address him.

"I cannot tell you my name," said the angel, "Because it is beyond your understanding. Trust only God, and all will be well."

Manoah then prepared an offering to make to the angel, but the angel was angry with him for this.

"Make only sacrifices to God, for He alone is worthy to receive them!" warned the angel. He then struck the offering that Manoah had brought with his stick, which caused it to burst into flames. The flames and the angel then disappeared, returning to heaven.

Manoah and his wife were so amazed at what they saw, that they no longer doubted that God had spoken to them through His angel. Yet, Manoah feared that his life was now in danger, for it was forbidden to have sight of God.

"We should not fear, my husband," his wife promised. "Had God not wanted us to witness this, then He would not have allowed it to happen. Let us go forth with joy, and look forward to the day when our child is born!"

So it was that in time, Samson was born. When he grew older, he took a vow as the angel had cautioned, promising that he would never take drinks that might lead him to drunkenness, nor cut his hair with a razor.

When he reached maturity, Samson decided to leave his parents for awhile, to travel around Israel, and to visit nearby lands. He came into the land of the Philistines, who were hostile toward Israel, and there he met a woman whom he wanted to be his wife.

To marry a Philistine was forbidden by his own people, but God had put this incurable love in Samson's heart for a reason, to enable him to ensnare this great enemy of Israel. So too, God had stirred a great passion within Samson for seeking justice, and filled him with great strength in his body. In fact, Samson was one of the strongest men who have ever lived, and there are many tales told that attest to this.

When he returned to his parents, Samson told them of his desire to marry the Philistine woman. Manoah and his wife were beside themselves when they heard what Samson wished for.

"This you cannot do!" they implored their son. "Our people are forbidden to marry any but from the tribes of Israel. To do otherwise would surely bring God's punishment upon us!"

Samson's parents begged him to change his mind, but their son was determined to marry the woman whom he loved.

"My love for her is a love that I cannot deny!" said Samson. "We are surely meant to be together! Come with me to meet her family, and you will see for yourself that I am right!"

Very reluctantly, Samson's parents agreed to journey with him, and to meet with the woman's parents, to see whether they might agree that their offspring may be married.

Along the way, and while out of sight of his parents, Samson was set upon by a desert lion.

Without breaking his stride, Samson turned around, seized the lion by its neck, and hurled it with great power onto the side of the path! He then set upon the lion himself, tearing it from limb to limb, as though he were plucking feathers from a chicken.

Samson continued his journey, but did not tell his parents what he had done. He again met the woman who had stolen his heart, and was consumed with even more love for her.

When he came back some later time, he noticed that a swarm of bees had taken home within the carcass of the very lion that he had struck to pieces.

Thinking that the bees' honey would make a fine meal for himself, and a suitable gift for his parents besides, Samson reached into the swarming mass, and took some of their perfectly-treated nectar.

Samson's wedding to the Philistine woman was then arranged, and her father gathered thirty local men to serve as his groomsmen.

When they were all seated at the wedding feast, Samson decided to present the young men with a riddle.

"I will tell you a riddle," began Samson. "If you can solve it within the seven days of our feast, I will give you thirty sets of clothes and fine linen. But if you cannot, you must give the same to me!"

"We love riddles!" responded the men excitedly. "Tell us yours, which we will surely easily solve!"

"Here then is the riddle that you must find the answer to," replied Samson:

"Out of the eater comes something to eat,
Out of the strong comes something that's sweet!"

The men scratched their heads, but could not fathom an answer to this most peculiar puzzle. Over three days, they debated among themselves what the strange words might mean, trying to make sense of what Samson had told them. Thinking then that he had cheated them in order to win possessions from them, they entreated his new wife to persuade him to reveal the secret to her.

While she was afraid, the men threatened to kill her if she did not obtain the answer.

"This riddle we must solve," demanded the men. "For if we do not, the Israelite will surely make a laughing stock of our people!"

The new bride cried bitterly for days. Only as the week-long celebration of their marriage was coming to a close, did she mention what was troubling her to her husband.

So it was, that Samson was then persuaded to explain the riddle's meaning.

The men were delighted with her devious work, and near the end of the seven days, came ready to reveal the answer to Samson.

"Bees in the carcass make sweet-tasting honey–

The carcass that remains of a lion that is strong!" they haughtily exclaimed.

Samson was furious that they had discovered the riddle's answer, knowing that it was his wife who must have told them. His anger burned ever stronger, but he knew that he must honor his promise, and bring them thirty suits of clothes, and thirty sets of fine linen.

So Samson stormed out of the house, and went to a town of the Philistines called Ashkelon, where he struck down thirty of the young men who lived there. Then he took from them their garments and linen, which he brought back for the groomsmen.

Samson then returned to his homeland, but without asking his wife to travel with him.

After a while, her father decided that Samson would not be returning to make strong their union, and that the time was then suitable for her to marry another man. This, it was proposed, should be one of the groomsmen who had been with Samson at the wedding party. A new wedding was quickly arranged, while Samson remained unaware that his wife was now wedded to another man.

Following several months, Samson decided to return to the land of the Philistines, to seek the company of his wife once more.

When he arrived at her father's house, he was furious to learn that she had remarried.

"For this, your family, and all your kin, must surely be punished!" bellowed Samson.

Filled with a burning rage, and with a courage stirred by God, Samson then charged into the fields, where he captured three hundred foxes. With his own hands, he tied each to another of its kind, such that in all, one hundred and fifty pairs were joined together: though each yearning to go their separate way.

Samson then lit a firebrand and took it to each of the foxes in turn, setting alight their tails, turning them into blazing torches.

Shrieking in pain, and struggling to be parted from the creature with which they were paired, the foxes tore through the countryside, setting alight all the crops. In very little time, everything that grew was burned to cinders, killing the harvest, and bringing misery to those who depended upon the crops for their food.

Men from among the Philistines soon learned that the great fire had been started because of Samson's rage, and sought retribution for his father-in-law and wife, who they believed had been the cause of such misery.

Following the foxes' rampage, Samson left the home of his former wife, and came to the land of Judah, where he rested in a cave.

In time, a delegation from Philistine came to the people of Judah, demanding that they hand over Samson to them.

"This we must do," promised the hosts, "For we trust what you tell us, that this man has killed many of your people."

So a large army of Judeans went to Samson's cave, and there insisted that he hand himself over to them.

"You may bind my hands with rope, and lead me to my enemy," promised Samson, "But you must not kill me yourselves!"

"We give you our word that we will not kill you!" assured the Judeans. "We will take you to meet the Philistine soldiers, and there God will decide your fate!"

Samson then allowed his hands to be bound with rope, and he was led through the desert to the place where the Philistine soldiers were camping.

As the party approached, Samson was filled with a strength that had rarely been witnessed before. He snapped apart the rope that had been tightly coiled around his wrists. Then spotting a donkey's jawbone that he might use as a weapon, he quickly picked it up, and then charged at the astonished Philistines, clubbing all around him with his makeshift weapon, killing all of one thousand men at a single time!

Following his remarkable display, Samson felt very thirsty, and he called upon God to lead him to water.

"My throat is dry from my heavy work," cried Samson. "Might it please my LORD to show me where I might find water that I can drink?"

God heard Samson's prayer, and immediately brought forth a spring of water, from which Samson could take his refreshment.

Such were the remarkable tales of Samson's daring and strength in facing the Philistines, that he was made Judge of Israel!

Samson traveled as he willed, often staying at the homes of different people.

One day, he rested with a woman in the land of Gaza. When his enemies got wind of his visit, they set about a plot to kill him.

"Let him rest with the woman until morning time," they chuckled, "Then he will be tired, and we will easily be able to set upon him!"

Samson rested with the woman for awhile, but was moved to leave her house early, even breaking down the gates of the city, along with the old, sturdy wooden beam that supported the city wall above them. Samson then carried these on his shoulders to the top of a hill close by.

The people marveled at what they saw, and could not reason how one man could acquire so much strength.

One other time, Samson came to the home of a woman, whose name was Delilah. His heart burned with love for her, and he planned to spend time in her company.

Seeing that Delilah might be able to charm Samson sufficiently for him to reveal to her the secret of his strength, a group of men who wished to kill him came to her, offering to pay her eleven hundred silver coins if she could bring her lover to tell his story.

Knowing that she would live handsomely for the rest of her life were she to come into possession of such riches, Delilah set about a plan to entice Samson to make known his secret.

"My dear lover," she began one night, after settling down to be beside her famous visitor. "Please tell me how you came to be so strong!"

Not being easily tempted, Samson whispered his reply, making up a false answer to tease the woman.

"That is easy to explain!" laughed Samson. "If anyone were to bind my hair with seven fresh bowstrings that have not yet been dried, then my strength will desert me, and I will become as feeble as any other man!"

Delilah kissed Samson on the cheek, and then sang softly to him, as he drifted slowly into a peaceful sleep.

When she heard him snoring and was sure that he was sleeping soundly, Delilah quickly rushed to find the men who had promised her the silver coins.

"It was so easy!" she excitedly exclaimed. "All anyone need do is tie his hair with seven fresh bowstrings that have never been dried. Then, he says, he will become as feeble as any other man!"

The men then hid themselves behind the curtains in the room where Samson was sleeping. Delilah took seven fresh bowstrings that had never been dried, and tied them around the locks of Samson's hair, just as he had described. She then let out a scream, meaning to wake him.

"Quick, Samson! Awake!" she cried. "There are men in the room, meaning to kill you!"

At her cry, Samson sat up in a flash, but simply tugged at the strange cords in his hair, freeing them in an instant, as easily as though he were snapping a stalk of corn in a field.

"Where are these men that you speak about?" he laughed. "If any are here, I will surely tear them limb from limb!"

When the men heard this, they were afraid, and did not move from their hiding places.

Delilah felt deceived, but she determined a second time to make Samson reveal his secret.

"My dear and most honorable beloved," she began the following evening, when they had again settled down to recline, after taking their meal. "Last night you made a fool of me by teasing me with your lies. I am embarrassed, but beg you my friend, to tell me the truth about your strength."

"It is not bowstrings that must bind my hair," replied Samson, "But only rope that has never been used before.

"If my seven braids are so tied, then my strength will escape me, and I will become as feeble as any other man!"

Delilah kissed Samson, and then again waited for him to fall asleep.

A second time, she called for the men who sought to kill him to enter the room, telling them the method by which Samson had said he could be caught, again beseeching them to hide in his chamber while he slept.

Taking seven new ropes, she then bound Samson's locks, as he had advised.

A second time, she cried out to him, "Samson! Wake quickly! There are men here, and they mean to kill you!"

Samson quickly awoke from his slumber. Immediately, he pinched apart each of the ropes that had curled in his hair, each of which came apart in his fingers just like flakes of melted candle wax break in the hands.

"Woman, I am not made a fool of so easily!" hollered Samson. Laughing to himself, he then fell back into a contented sleep.

Delilah's face flushed red with embarrassment, knowing that she could not humor the patience of the men who wanted to kill Samson for much longer.

On the third night, she again implored Samson to tell his secret.

"What one who would break my power must do is this," he began. "My hair must be tied to the fabric that stretches out on a loom, and then fastened with a pin! Any who succeed in catching me in such a way will render me powerless, and I will become as feeble as any other man!"

As she had before, Delilah related what Samson had told her to the men, then had one of her servants fetch a loom to which she might tie Samson's hair, just as he had related to her.

One more time, while he was sleeping, Delilah cried out to him.

"They are here again!" she shouted. "The men who want to kill you are here, prowling around, and jealous for your blood!"

Samson woke quickly, but again surprised Delilah and the men who watched from the shadows with his strength, freeing himself from the loom with the least effort, then hurling the loom into the corner of the room, where it broke into many pieces.

"Now let me return to my sleep!" screamed Samson. "No more of your crazy interruptions!"

Delilah wept inconsolably for days, berating Samson for making such a fool of her. Still, she did not give in from seeking to discover the secret of his great power.

"If only you tell me the truth, and I know that I can trust you, will I be happy," Delilah pleaded with Samson. "Do not make a fool of me any longer, for I will never again be able to lift my head up to the sun if you do so!"

Fearing that Delilah's distress might lead her to madness, Samson eventually decided to tell her the truth.

"I have been untruthful to you until now," he said, making clear that this time he did not intend to make a fool of his beloved companion.

"This is the real secret of my strength. I made a vow to God when I was a boy that I would never allow my hair to be cut with a razor. Were anyone to do this, I would lose my strength, and I would truly become as feeble as any other man!"

Samson then kissed Delilah, and settled onto his couch, where he soon fell into a deep sleep.

Seeing that this time, Samson seemed sincere, Delilah went to fetch the men one more time, revealing what Samson had told her. She then called for a servant to be brought to her with a razor and shaving soap. While Samson was sleeping, the servant stripped him of his glorious seven locks of hair!

"Samson! Wake up! The men are here!" shrieked Delilah, as she had three times before.

Samson sat up, believing that he would again be able to resist the attempts of any intruder to subdue him. However, he realized that this time, his strength had deserted him.

The men came out from their hiding places, and then bound Samson in chains. They took him to Gaza, where he was set to work grinding grain.

Even as his hair was growing back, still he could not escape. This is because his captors had gouged out his eyes, and bound his legs with bronze shackles.

Samson knew that Delilah had deceived him. But even in his prison, he did not give up believing that God would bring about justice for those who had bound and blinded him.

It came to pass that a great celebration was called by the Philistines to honor their god, Dagon, whom they believed had delivered Samson into their hands.

"Let us all gather to give thanks to our great god!" decreed the rulers of the Philistines. "Let us make sacrifices and sing praises to the one who has delivered us from the Israelite, from the one who has slayed many hundreds of our kin!"

Preparations were then made for the celebration, and many thousands of people gathered at the temple of Dagon, their leaders and esteemed elders among them.

So large was the crowd that gathered, that many even clambered onto the roof of the temple, hoping that by being there, they might at least be able to hear what was happening below.

In the middle of the celebration, some of the people called out, suggesting that Samson be paraded before them and coaxed into performing for their entertainment.

So it was, that Samson was brought out from his prison, and made to entertain the braying throng.

The people laughed and stamped their feet, mocking Samson, and hurling many abuses at him.

When he had performed for a while, Samson begged one of his guards to allow him to rest against one of the columns of the temple, so that he might collect his breath. His hair had been regrowing, but he knew that God alone could restore the strength that he once had.

"Mighty God," pleaded Samson. "Give me strength one more time to reveal Your justice to this evil people. Do not allow the cruelty that they have inflicted on Your servant to go unpunished!"

Trusting that God would not desert him, Samson then stretched out his arms, with one hand resting upon one of the main pillars at the centre of the temple, and his other upon another.

With a loud cry, he called out to God one more time. "Bring down this temple, and crush all who are within it, even Your servant, Samson!"

Stretching wide his arms to push against each pillar with all the might that he could summon, Samson was then filled with the strength that he had once known. God restored his full power, coming to His servant in his time of most need.

Then the pillars began to crack. With one final heave, each snapped into two, bringing the roof of the temple crashing down on top of all the people who were within it.

Samson died crying out to God, but knowing that justice had been done.

His family later took his body, and buried him at the same place where his father now lay.

This great leader and warrior for God had ruled in Israel for a full twenty years. Now he rests in heaven, where God continues to provide for his every need.

CHAPTER EIGHT

The Story of Ruth, The Faithful

MANY YEARS AGO, in a land known as Judah, there lived a man named Elimelek. Along with his wife Naomi, Elimelek had two sons, who were called Mahlon and Kilion. Times were hard in Judah, because a famine had plagued the land for many months. No crops could grow, and many animals were dying for lack of food and water.

Since they were close to starving, Elimelek decided to move his family many miles to the kingdom of Moab, a land that was said to be fertile, although its people had once been unkind to the inhabitants of Judah.

Still, Elimelek felt that he had no choice. He then led his small family from their home in Bethlehem across the desert, and over to the far side of a large body of water known as the Dead Sea into the land of the Moabites.

Life was not easy for Elimelek's family, but now they at least had food to eat. And so they settled in Moab, planning to make this strange and faraway land their new home.

Further tragedy was to befall this family, for Elimelek soon died, leaving his wife Naomi a widow, forced to bring up her two sons alone.

Naomi loved her sons, and wanted for them to be happy. When the time came for them to marry, she was content to know that they both found wives, who were from Moabite families–some say even from a royal family, although this we may never know.

The wives' names were Orpah and Ruth. Both were kind and beautiful, honoring their new family as though it were the one to which they had been born.

For a short time, Naomi was happy. But sad times were to fall upon her and her offspring once more.

Within a short time of their being married, both Mahlon and Kilion died, leaving their mother childless and her two daughter-in-laws without husbands.

In those times, it was hard for young women to earn a living for themselves, for men owned the land and commanded the best jobs. Yet, Orpah and Ruth worked very hard, tilling the land, and always showing kindness to their mother-in-law.

Naomi saw that Orpah and Ruth loved her dearly, but she longed to return to her homeland.

In time, news reached Naomi that the famine that had affected Judah had now passed. Believing that the time was right to return, she begged her daughter-in-laws to give up their duties of caring for her, beseeching them to find new husbands from among the men of their own people.

"My children, it is time for me to make the long journey back across the desert to the town of Bethlehem, my true home!" announced Naomi. "This I must do, to be reunited with my own kin. But you too must now make your lives with those of your own people. Find yourselves new husbands, and may you prosper and live long lives!"

Orpah and Ruth were distraught to hear Naomi's plan, for they loved her dearly, and did not wish to be parted from her.

"You are as a mother to us!" the girls proclaimed. "How can we ever contemplate being apart? Ours is a joy and an honor to serve you. Let us travel with you to this far away land, even though we may never see our homeland any more!"

"My daughters, don't leave your homes! Stay with those who know you–your brothers, uncles, cousins, and kinsfolk. They will surely grieve deeply if you leave with me, and there will be husbands for you here, with whom you can make new lives.

"If you stay with me, you will remain widows and childless. I am now unable to bear further sons, and even were I to do so today, it would be many years before my offspring would be old enough to serve as your husbands! Again, my beloveds, I beg you to allow me to go my own way!"

Orpah and Ruth were beside themselves with Naomi's pronouncement. They shed many tears, and continued to offer themselves in her service, even beginning on the journey with her toward her homeland.

Eventually, as Naomi continued her pleas, Orpah decided that her mother-in-law was right, that they should part and seek new lives in their different homelands.

"Beloved mother-in-law, while my heart is very heavy with grief, I now see that we must part," cried Orpah." I will do as you say, returning to my homeland to find a new husband. Yet I will always hold your memory in my heart. Travel well, my gracious matron, and may God be kind to you when you come again to your distant land!"

The two women embraced for many moments, shedding many tears, for they knew that they might never meet again.

Yet Ruth would not move from her position.

"My dear mother-in-law," she began, "It is my honor and duty to serve you, and especially now that your sons have gone. You know that my heart is filled with love for you, and I will follow you wherever you travel. I cannot be happy unless I am serving you. And to see you happy is what brings me most joy!"

"Let me continue to accompany you on this long journey. Together, we will cross mountain passes and wander over desert sands. I am your servant, dear mother-in-law, and will remain so while we both have breath!"

Naomi tried again to persuade Ruth that her plan was the most sensible one, but Ruth could not be tempted to change her mind. And so eventually, Naomi conceded, and accepted Ruth's determination to accompany her on her journey home.

The road back to Bethlehem was not an easy one, but when they arrived, Naomi and Ruth learned that more profitable times had returned to the land of Judah. Even when they came into the town, a new harvest was being gathered.

Naomi was barely recognizable to those who had once known her, since she was frail after her long journeying and her meager existence in Moab, and her skin furrowed with countless lines after the many years of grief and worry that she had suffered.

"Is this our neighbor Naomi, who once dwelt among us?" cried the people when she passed through the town gate. "Surely this is her, although she appears so weathered and fraught."

"It is I," replied Naomi, "Although do not call me by the name that you know, but now know me as Mara, which means bitterness, as my life has become one of trial, misfortune, and sadness."

Very soon after they arrived in Bethlehem, Ruth enjoined her mother-in-law to allow her to go into the fields, where she might follow behind the women who were gathering up the barley stalks, in case she could glean any loose leaves that they left behind them.

And so Ruth went into the field outside the town, which belonged to a man named Boaz.

Ruth labored all day, scarcely taking a break to drink water, gathering what she could. Silently, and without complaint, she worked, trailing behind the other women, gathering what they did not want, and the remnants of what the wind blew from their hands.

Close to noontime, when the sun reaches its highest point in the sky, Boaz passed by the women with his men on their way to lunch, and noticed Ruth following behind.

"Who is this young woman that follows in your tail?" he asked.

"She is the child from the land of Moab who came with Naomi back to our land," the women replied.

"Come here child," Boaz beckoned to Ruth.

Nervously, but without hesitation, Ruth came before Boaz, bowing her head low in front of him.

"Do not be afraid!" began Boaz. "I have heard what a good servant you have been to Naomi, tending for her during her many years of grief, never leaving her side. You are an honorable woman, one who never fails in duty, and surely God must smile kindly upon you!

"Continue to work in my fields. I will ensure that no harm comes to you, and see to it that you are treated well. At lunch, I will serve you grain, and you may take what you gather back to Naomi with my blessing!"

With a trembling voice, and still bowing low, Ruth offered her gratitude to this worthy man.

"My Lord, how do I deserve such kindness? I am a child of Moab, yet you treat me as though I were a daughter from your own kingdom! I am truly blessed, although I am the least among your workers. May you be greatly honored and praised!"

As he had promised, Boaz gave Ruth grain at lunch, and after she had eaten a little, he beseeched her to keep the remainder as a gift for her mother-in-law, so that Ruth would not return home without anything.

And too, Boaz commanded his men to deal kindly with Ruth, and to allow her to follow behind the other women, even insisting that they take some stalks for her from their own bundles for her to include among her own.

Ruth labored until the sun set, then returned to Naomi with what she had gathered, which amounted to almost a sackful of barley!

Naomi questioned where Ruth had worked, and was delighted to hear that this was a field owned by Boaz, who was a close relative of hers.

"This man is known for his kindness and fairness," said Naomi. "How fortuitous it is that you were led to him. Go to his field tomorrow, for he will surely watch over you, and ensure that you come to no harm!"

Ruth did as her mother-in-law advised, continuing to work hard in Boaz's fields until all the harvest had been gathered.

Naomi sought Boaz's protection for her daughter-in-law, and for herself too. When she heard that Boaz would be spending a night at his threshing floor, where his men would be winnowing the grain, she urged Ruth to go to him, but not to make herself known until he was sleeping.

"Dress yourself in your finest clothes, and put on perfume," Naomi advised. "When my relative is sleeping and all others have left for their beds, go and lie down beside his feet, but do not allow the drape of his garment to cover either his feet nor your body."

"My dear mother-in-law," replied Ruth, "While I do not understand the meaning in your plan, you know that I trust you completely. I will do as you say."

Ruth then prepared herself as her mother-in-law had instructed, putting on her finest dress and perfume. She then rushed to the threshing floor where Boaz and his men were working, and waited until they had had their supper and were making merry conversation.

When the men departed and Boaz lay down to sleep, Ruth did as her mother-in-law had told. She lay down at the foot of Boaz, uncovering his feet. And there she rested, as Naomi had promised her that Boaz would then tell her what to do.

After some time, Boaz awoke, and saw that a young woman was lying at his feet.

"What are you doing here, my child?" he calmly enquired.

"My master, it is your servant Ruth. Please, allow your coat to cover my side also, for I hear that you are a guardian to our family."

"My child, I will protect you," answered Boaz. "Move closer, and allow the hem of my garment to cover you. You may stay here tonight, but you must rise early, for others must not know that you were here!

"I offer you my word, I will always honor your family. But there is one who has a greater claim than I to the honor of being your guardian. Tomorrow, I will look for him, and if he deems to be your guardian and wishes to redeem you, then his will must take precedent. However, if he is not forthcoming, I will surely do so in his stead!"

Ruth remained at Boaz's side until dawn, when he ordered her to spread out her shawl, in order that he could pour six measures of barley onto it.

"Take these to your dear mother-in-law with my blessing!" said Boaz. And then he departed for the town.

Ruth returned to Naomi's home, where she presented the gift of barley to her, and told her everything that had happened.

"Boaz will surely be very focused on this matter," assured Naomi. "Wait here now until we learn what happens today!"

Boaz, meantime, had rushed to the town, where he came upon the man who had a greater claim than he to be guardian to Naomi's family. Such that he may have witnesses, as was the tradition among his people, Boaz also called upon the elders of the town to gather with them.

"My friend, it is time that the matter of protection for Naomi and her family is decided. She is selling land that belongs to her late husband, Elimelek. It is for you to decide first whether to purchase this land, and with this the family title and guardianship of their descendants and servants. Before the witnesses gathered here, will you take this land?"

"I will do so without hesitation!" replied the man. "Naomi will come under my protection, although she no longer has offspring to continue the family line."

"This is not so, my neighbor," continued Boaz. "For the Moab daughter Ruth is a part of her household, and the widow of one of her sons besides. She must also be protected, for to fail to do so would be to deny our relative Elimelek his right of inheritance!"

"Then this I cannot do!" responded the man. "For me to become a guardian for a Moab woman would surely bring dishonor upon my family, and lead to misfortune! May you, as next in line with a right to this title, buy this land and take Naomi and the Moab girl into your protection. In the presence of witnesses, I pass on my right to you!"

The man then removed his sandal and passed it to Boaz. This was a tradition at the time, showing one person's commitment to respect their agreement. And so it was that Boaz was able to purchase the land, and take Naomi and Ruth into his protection.

"I will take Ruth as my wife," announced Boaz, "For by doing so, the family name of her departed husband and his father Elimelek will not die!"

The elders who were gathered as witnesses offered their congratulations to Boaz.

"May Ruth bring blessings to your home as Rachel and Leah did before her!" they exclaimed. "May her offspring always be blessed, and seed a family line that grows and prospers through many generations!"

Boaz then married Ruth, and within a short time, she gave birth to a son.

The women who were close to Naomi told her, "Blessed are you, dear woman, for you have obtained the protection of a worthy man! Now he is husband to your daughter-in-law, and so too, your family name is protected!

"May this child be blessed, and may he become famous in our nation! He gives you life anew, and will support you in your old age. Blessed is your daughter-in-law Ruth, who through her faithful service to you and selfless laboring, has made possible this miracle. Surely, she is worth more to you than are even seven sons!"

Naomi then took the child into her arms, and cradled him. Now she shed tears of joy, and loved her daughter-in-law all the more.

The boy was named Obed, who in turn became the father of Jesse, whose own son David in turn became king of a great nation.

CHAPTER NINE

The Tale of David and Goliath, and David and Saul

MANY YEARS AGO, there lived a man named David, who grew up to become a much loved king of an ancient country called Israel. At that time, David's people were often fighting with their neighbors, and especially with their long-time enemies, who were known as the Philistines.

However, David did not become king by being the son of the reigning king of Israel, who at the time of David's birth was King Saul. In fact, David was not a prince at all when he was born, and he was the youngest of his father's eight sons.

Saul had been chosen to be the first king of his country, but he had soon started to disobey God. After his army won an important battle, he even set up a monument to honor himself rather than God.

God spoke to his servant Samuel, who was a great priest of the people of Israel at the time, one of a small number of people known as prophets, who passed messages from God to the people.

Samuel came to Saul and told him that God was angry with him, because he had not carried out His instructions. But Saul pretended that he had been faithful to God.

Samuel was very wise, and knew that Saul was not telling the truth. So, he spoke very strongly to the king, warning him that God was angry with him because he had lied. Samuel turned around to leave Saul, but Saul pulled on the hem of Samuel's cloak, tearing off a piece of it.

"Because you have done this," said Samuel, "God Himself will take away the kingdom of Israel from you, and give it to one of your neighbors!"

Samuel stayed with Saul for a brief time after giving God's warning, and for a brief time too, Saul was sorry to God for what he had done, and offered his praises to Him. But soon Samuel left him, never to speak with him again.

While Samuel was very angry with Saul for what he had done, he still loved him, and was very sad that he had turned away from being a good king who had once been faithful to his Lord.

God then spoke to Samuel, telling him to go to a tiny town called Bethlehem, which was home to a man named Jesse. God told Samuel that one of Jesse's sons would one day become king of Israel, and that he was to go there to find him. David was one of Jesse's many sons.

David was then young, and too young to go to war, as was the duty of his elder brothers.

Instead, David watched over his father's sheep, making sure that they did not come to any harm from wolves and lions and the many other wild beasts that roamed the countryside. While he was still very young, David loved God and was not afraid to be alone in the fields after dark, nor to ward off any wild animals that came his way.

When Samuel arrived in Bethlehem, the people were surprised to see him and afraid of what he may tell them, for he was well-known as being a powerful servant of God, who often brought warnings that they did not want to hear.

Samuel promised the people that he had come to their village in peace, and invited Jesse and his sons to join him in a ceremony to give praise to God. In this way, he thought that he could come to know Jesse's sons, and learn which of them was destined to become king of Israel.

First, Samuel cast his eyes upon the eldest son of Jesse, who stood proudly before him, full of confidence.

"Surely this will be the new king!" thought Samuel. But God spoke to Samuel's heart, and told him that this was not to be.

Then Jesse presented the second eldest of his sons, who, like his elder brother, was physically very strong and spoke with clever words and had many ingenious ideas and plans.

"Now you must be the one that God has chosen!" reasoned Samuel. But God again told him that this was not to be so.

Jesse then introduced his third son, who like his elder brothers, had proved to be a worthy hero in battle. But again, God told Samuel that this was not His chosen one.

All in all, Jesse presented his seven eldest sons to Samuel, but God said that none of these was to become king.

"Surely you have no other sons?" questioned Samuel, when the seven of Jesse's offspring stood before him.

"Well, there is one more," replied Jesse. "But he is very young, and I have set him to work, tending my sheep."

At first, Samuel was doubtful that the Lord could have such a young man in mind to become leader of such a great nation. But God told him, "People always look to outward appearances when they judge whether one may be worthy or not for a task. Yet I always look at the heart, for this is where a person's true character can be found!"

So Samuel requested that Jesse send for his youngest son to be brought to him, who was the shepherd boy called David.

When David arrived, Samuel could see that he had a glowing light and a warmth about him that reflected the love that was in his heart. He was handsome too, and in the finest health.

"This is the one who will be king of Israel!" declared God, "My precious son, David."

And so, Samuel called David forward to him, and told him that he was to become a great leader. As a mark of God's favor, Samuel took a little oil and anointed David with this on his forehead. From that time forward, David's love for God grew and grew, and God guided him, and made him wise.

However, God no longer watched over Saul as he had before, and when God's close presence departed from him, Saul became ill and was constantly tormented. Seeing how troubled he was by this, one of Saul's servants suggested that someone should be brought to him who could play sweet and melodious music, which might help relieve the king from his torment.

Saul liked this plan, and so gave orders that the most gifted harp player in the land be found and brought to him.

Now, it was known that David could play the harp very beautifully. His bravery and friendly charms were also often spoken about, and many people spoke of his love for his Lord, and the comfort that they felt when they were close to him.

Saul then sent out his messengers to find David, and to instruct Jesse to send his son to the royal court. Jesse blessed his son, and sent him on his way to the palace on a donkey, carrying with him bread, some wine, and a young goat to offer as a gift to the king.

David quickly became very popular in the court. He delighted Saul with his music and charming manner, and his beautiful music soon helped calm Saul's torment. So, Saul made him his armour bearer, and willed that David would continue to stay with him.

While he was serving in Saul's court, David was from time to time allowed to return to his home in Bethlehem to see his father, and to help him tend his sheep.

On one occasion, the time was coming near for Saul's military men to once again fight the Philistines. Jesse had sent his three eldest sons to join the army, and asked David to take bread for them, as well as cheeses for their general.

"I beg you, my dear son, to bring me news that your brothers are safe," said Jesse. "May God protect you on your journey, and may you return home quickly, bringing good news!"

At the place where Saul's army was gathering, there was much trepidation and fear. Saul had gathered his force on one side of a valley, on top of a great hill. The Philistines had gathered on top of a hill on the other side, facing them from across the valley.

Saul was worried because one of the Philistines, a giant man named Goliath, had challenged him to present a single man to fight with him.

Now Goliath was truly a giant–nearly ten feet tall, and he wore a breastplate and skirt of armour that alone weighed as much as many of the men in Saul's army. His mighty sword was six times heavier than a normal sword, and he roared like a fearless lion, terrifying everyone with his loud and fearless voice.

Saul, and all of his army, felt certain that there was no one among them who would be a suitable match for Goliath. Yet the giant kept telling them, "Let just one man from among you fight me, you cowards! If he strikes me dead, then you will win the battle, and this land and our possessions will be yours! But if you lose, then you will become the slaves to my people!"

The two armies faced each other for forty full days across the valley. Each day, Goliath came to the front of his ranks and bellowed his invitation. Each day, Saul and his army cowered in fear, not knowing how to respond.

David soon completed his journey from Bethlehem, and found his brothers among the gathering soldiers of the Israelites. He brought them the bread that his father had sent for them, and offered the gift of cheeses to their commander.

While David was with them, Goliath again came out onto the hilltop and shouted out his challenge.

David asked his eldest brother what Goliath wanted, and saw that the army of Saul was afraid. Angry that David was asking questions but was himself too young to fight, his brother rebuked him.

"You come here just to watch what is going on!" shouted his brother, "While we are the ones who must risk our lives for our country. Go back home, where you belong, among the sheep! This is no place for onlookers!"

David left his brother alone, but continued his questioning. Again, the soldiers whom he spoke with told him to be gone. One of Saul's guards who was close by overheard their angry conversation. He rushed to tell Saul, who commanded that David be brought to him.

When David came before Saul, he humbled himself, and saluted the king.

"My great master! I have heard that your army is afraid because of the demands of the giant called Goliath!" began David. "Do not be afraid! I will step forward to fight your enemy!" David promised.

Saul looked at David with deep concern in his eyes, as he was certain that David was fooling himself to believe that he could survive even for a moment in the face of this terrible giant.

"My servant, you are very valiant and full of courage, but too young to face this evil aggressor!" said Saul. "We would be quickly defeated, and then we will all become slaves to the Philistines!"

David listened carefully to Saul's words, but he was not dissuaded from his intended course of action.

"I may appear as a young shepherd boy to you," started David, "And I have never fought in battle before. But I have tended my father's sheep with a love that a father has for his sons, and risked my life many times before for their sakes. I have fought lions, and bears, and wolves, and all manner of wild animals that have frightened my flock.

"I have tugged on the manes of lions and gouged their eyes out! I have set traps for prowling bears, and brought them tumbling down without lifting my finger! To fight Goliath will be no different for me, and I know that I will win, because God is on my side!"

Saul was very troubled by David's proposal, but he could see that he was very insistent, and knew too that God had always protected David before. So, very reluctantly, he agreed that David should represent his army against the mighty Goliath.

"May God be with you, brave David!" said Saul. "I will give you my own tunic, and my sword and shield to protect you."

David put on the tunic and helmet that Saul gave to him, and strapped a harness over his shoulder to support his sword. But David had never worn a suit of armour before, which felt very heavy for him, and he found it hard to move. So he told Saul that he would fight the giant without armour.

David then went down the hill to where a stream was flowing, and collected five smooth and shiny stones from the water's edge. He put these into his pouch, and took with him a sling. Then he prepared to step forward to face the terrifying giant.

When he saw the man that the Israelites had chosen to fight him, Goliath let out a huge, menacing laugh.

"O you foolish people!" he bellowed. "How easily victory will come to me!"

Goliath saw that David was very young, although he was handsome and full of courage.

"Young man, I will tear your flesh from your bones!" laughed the giant. "You come to me with sticks and stones, as though I were a dog! But it is you who will soon become food for the birds and wild animals!"

Goliath continued laughing, but David was not daunted by the giant's taunting.

"You have a mighty shield, a javelin, and a sword to fight me," answered David. "But I have the support of God Almighty! Today, it will be you who is slain, and I will carry your head high above my shoulders. You, who have for a long time now cried out abuses and threats towards God's people, will this day make your own people slaves to the people of Israel!"

This made Goliath very angry, and he charged toward David, meaning to strike him down in an instant.

However, David was too quick for him. He reached for a stone from his pouch, and swung it straight at the forehead of Goliath, which was uncovered by armour. The stone buried deep into the giant's head, killing him in an instant. With this one strike, Goliath fell backward onto the ground, where David rushed to tower over him, then cutting off the giant's head, and holding it high above his shoulders.

The Philistines were astonished by what they saw. Now it was their turn to be afraid. They turned to run, but Saul and his army quickly followed them, killing many, and taking their possessions.

When the fighting was over, David came to Saul, who was amazed at what he had seen. Certain that it was God Who had, through His servant David, won the battle, Saul enjoined David to remain with him in his court.

Saul's own son Jonathan became a close friend of David, even giving his own tunic and sword to his new friend. David loved Jonathan, as though he were a brother, and knew that he would faithfully always stand by him, and tell him the truth.

David joined Saul's army, and pleased Saul in everything that he did, quickly being promoted to a high rank. Yet the king was less pleased when he saw that many of his own people started to love David more than he thought they loved himself.

"Saul has killed thousands," cried the people as Saul's army returned from the battlefront. "But David has killed tens of thousands!"

Hearing this made Saul become very angry. "Soon this young man will want my very kingdom!" he lamented, and from that day forward, he became suspicious of David, and started to watch him very carefully.

One day, while David was playing his harp to soothe the king's torment, Saul threw into a rage, and hurled his spear towards David, meaning to kill him. But David quickly saw what was happening, and managed to avoid being struck. A second time, Saul tried to pin David against the wall with his sword, but again David managed to avoid being hit.

Saul was amazed at David's quick movements, and felt certain that God was protecting him. So he made him a general in his army. David soon proved to be a successful and much loved leader. The people in the kingdom loved David, and praised him for being the savior of their land.

This made Saul even more afraid of David. So he decided to offer his eldest daughter to David in marriage, hoping that by becoming a member of his family, David would bring God's love and protection for all of the royal household.

David bowed low before the king, hailing him for his generous proposal, yet he refused to be wed.

"I am just a poor shepherd," said David. "How unsuitable am I to be a worthy husband for a king's daughter. Surely, this must be the destiny of a man from a wealthy family?"

So, the king's eldest daughter was married to another man.

However, another daughter of Saul, whose name was Michal, felt great love for David, and came to her father, imploring him to propose her as the young shepherd boy's wife.

This time, the king spoke with his servants, telling them to speak calmly with David, and to persuade him that he was well loved within the royal household, and that the king's greatest desire was that he became his son-in-law.

Again, David replied that he was unworthy to become a prince, and that his family could not afford a suitable wedding gift for a king's daughter.

Hearing this, Saul replied to his servants, "Tell David that all I require as a gift is one hundred skins from the backs of the Philistines, for I seek revenge on my enemies!"

Saul's servants again sought out David to make known the king's demand. But what they did not know was that the king really wanted David to face great danger in fighting the Philistines, hoping indeed that he might come to harm, or even be killed.

However, David decided to take his men into battle, and once more, was victorious against the Philistines. Not just one hundred, but two hundred skins he brought back to the king.

Saul now realized that God always protected David, and this made him even more afraid of him than before. When he saw the gift that David had brought him and remembered his promise, Saul called his daughter before him, and told her that her wish was granted, that she was to be David's bride. And so David and Michal were married.

David continued to be a great and popular leader of his troops, winning many famous battles. With his success, he became all the more loved by the people, who often cried out their praises to him whenever he passed by.

Seeing how popular David had become, Saul became more and more jealous of him. He hatched new plans to kill him, even asking his son Jonathan to search for David and slay him. But Jonathan remembered his promise to David, and rather than do as his father wished, he helped David to escape. David's wife Michael too got wind of her father's plans, and helped David to escape.

David traveled many miles, and rested in many places while Saul continued to pursue him.

At last, David came to a hiding place in an oasis town now known as En Gedi, where he found a cave to hide within.

Even here, David was not safe. Some of the local people betrayed his hiding place to Saul, who soon came looking for David, bringing his army with him.

Saul came to En Gedi, but didn't know precisely where David might be. Wishing to relieve himself, Saul walked into a cave, at the place that was also called the 'Crags of the Wild Goats'. This was the very cave in which David and some of his men were hiding!

Saul did not see David in the cave when he came inside, for it was very dark, and he had not yet had time to adjust his eyes so that he might see in the darkness. Carefully, and without making a sound, David crept up behind the King, and cut off a corner of his robe.

Saul was terrified to see David, accompanied by his men, but David ordered his men not to kill Saul, and permitted the king to leave the cave.

Then David came out from the cave and bowed down in front of the king.

"My master!" cried David, "You are my king, the one anointed as leader of Israel. Why do you believe that I wish to harm you? Today, you have seen that I might easily have struck you down when God brought you into the cave. Yet, this I did not do, for I know that you are anointed as our king!"

David showed Saul the corner of his robe that he had cut off, declaring, "This alone is what I took from you when the very knife that cut this cloth could have wounded your body! I did no wrong to you. Now, it is for God to judge between us. If I have done wrong, then God will judge me and punish me!"

When Saul heard this, he was deeply affected. Seeing that David had spared his life, he wept aloud.

"You are an honorable man, David, my son," said the king. "Now I know that you will one day be king, and that God is always by your side. I have done wrong against you."

David saw that the King was sorry, and they both made peace and went their separate ways.

However, it was not long before Saul again became jealous of David, and once more decided to kill him. He learned that David had come across the desert to a place called Ziph, so Saul again assembled his army and set off to find David.

When Saul came to Ziph, David's scouts told him that the king had set up camp close by and was preparing to hunt him down and kill him. David found out where the king was sleeping, and at nighttime, crept into the camp, where he saw Saul's spear planted into the ground right beside the king's head. A friend of David had come with him too, who wanted to thrust his spear into the king's body. But David urged him not to do this, reminding him that Saul was the anointed king of Israel.

Instead, David and his friend took Saul's spear and a water jug that was beside him, then left the camp. No one saw them, for God had caused the men in the camp to fall into a deep sleep.

When they were outside the camp, David called out to the commander of Saul's army, "Why didn't you guard your master, who is the anointed king of Israel?"

Holding high the water jug and the king's spear so that they could be seen, David continued, "Someone came to kill your king, taking his spear and water jug, that rested right beside his head. Yet you did not protect him even then. For this, you will surely die!"

Saul had now woken, and heard David's voice. When he realized that David had again spared his life when he could have killed him, Saul was very sorry for what he had done, and pleaded with David to forgive him.

As they had before in front of the cave, David and Saul agreed to be friends, and went their separate ways.

Still, David believed that Saul would not give up his jealousy for long, and soon would come hunting for him once more. So David decided to go far away from him, and came to hide in safety in the land of the Philistines.

It was not long before the Philistines set to war against Israel once more. This time Saul and three of his sons were killed in battle.

Soon after this terrible day, David was anointed as king by one of the tribes of Israel, and following the death of the fourth son of Saul, he became king over all of Israel.

David reigned for forty years, becoming one of the most famous and most loved kings of all time.

After winning more battles, he made Jerusalem his capital, and composed many beautiful songs to God, which are known as psalms. David remembered and thanked God for always protecting him and loving him. This we should also do, for God also loves and protects you and me.

CHAPTER TEN

Solomon, The Wise and The Wealthy

KING DAVID, a powerful and righteous king of Israel, lived until he was very old. During his final days, he could barely stand, and so he spent much of his time in his bedchamber. Poor David often found his body shivering, as he easily felt the cold.

When he saw that his father was close to dying, David's fourth eldest son Adonijah decided that the time had arrived for him to declare himself king. Adonijah then brought together many of the priests and high officials of the kingdom, along with the commander of the army, quickly mustering their support in aid of his claim to the crown.

These powerful men gathered with Adonijah, where they prepared a grand feast and sacrificed many animals in a ceremony to pronounce him as their new king.

However, some of King David's loyal servants were not invited to the celebration, including Zadok, the high priest, Nathan, the prophet, and David's favored son, Solomon.

Solomon had been chosen by David to be his successor. So, when his mother Bathsheba heard about Adonijah's plot to inherit the crown, denying Solomon from becoming king, she hurried to consult with Nathan, to decide what should be done.

"Go quickly to your husband, the king," urged Nathan. "Tell him that Adonijah has declared himself king, even before our beloved Majesty David has taken his last breath.

"Ask the king whether or not it is true that he promised that Solomon should be his successor. Ask whether the king has since changed his mind."

Nathan advised Bathsheba that he would wait outside the king's bedchamber while she consulted with him. Then he would make his presence known, confirming to the king that Adonijah had already appointed himself in Solomon's place.

Bathsheba then did as Nathan advised. She hurried to her husband's bedchamber, where she prostrated herself before the king.

Tales of Old

"Mighty Lord, have you not promised that my son Solomon shall be your chosen successor?" she enquired. "Is he not the one who is destined to protect our nation, and lead us to ever greater victories and prosperity?"

"This is my command, and my heart's desire," replied the king. "Soon, Solomon will sit upon my throne, and I will know that my kingdom has passed into trusted hands."

"O mighty king!" Bathsheba cried, "While you have been lying here, your son Adonijah has already proclaimed himself king. Even now, many of your Majesty's officials are with him, celebrating his new appointment. They have sacrificed many animals, and pledged their support to him.

"Now I fear that the future will be difficult for Solomon and myself. The new king will surely make us his servants, and your heart's wish that Solomon should be your heir may never come to be!"

At that moment, the king's guard announced the arrival of Nathan the prophet, who sought an urgent audience with David. Nathan was then shown into the king's bedchamber, where he described the events concerning Adonijah that Bathsheba had also spoken about.

"My king and glorious Majesty!" Nathan began, bowing low before the king. "Your servant is greatly troubled, for we have received news that your son Adonijah has declared himself to be king. Even now, many of your officials are gathered with him, sacrificing animals, and celebrating a rich feast, to claim him as their new ruler!

"Has Your Majesty not declared that your beloved son Solomon should be king after you? Might there have been a change to Your Majesty's wishes, or something that I and your noble wife Bathsheba are not aware of?"

When he heard what was happening, the king was very distressed. With great difficulty, he raised himself from his bed, then addressed his wife and his servant Nathan very severely.

"What you have told me is news to me!" uttered the king. "You have stated correctly that Solomon is my chosen heir. By my word, he will become king!

"Now I command that you take Solomon and anoint him as king. Adonijah will soon learn that my command has been obeyed. Take Solomon on a mule, and dress him in my royal robes. When you have anointed him, accompany him back to my palace, where he shall sit upon my throne!"

Nathan then did as the king ordered. Solomon was taken on a mule to a place where he was proclaimed king. Many priests and high officials joined the party, sounding their trumpets, and crying out excitedly in honor of their new king.

When he heard the loud cries and trumpet calls coming from the place where Solomon was anointed, Adonijah demanded to know what the commotion was about.

"That is the cry of those celebrating the anointing of Solomon as the new king of Israel," said one of the men who had witnessed Solomon's ceremony, and who had come quickly to bring news to Adonijah.

"King David himself issued his word that Solomon shall be his successor, and instructed his servant Nathan and Zadok the priest to ensure that this would come to be.

"Even now, the new king has been installed upon the throne, and is celebrating in the royal palace."

When Adonijah heard this news, he was distraught, for he knew that he had acted wrongly. He bowed low at the altar of God, begging that his life might be spared.

Solomon then forgave his brother, promising that if he remained faithful to God, he would not touch a hair on his body. Adonijah then returned to his home, and Solomon began what would become a famous reign.

Knowing that he was close to his end, King David gave his blessing to Solomon.

"Honor our ancestors, but first pledge your allegiance to God," David advised his son. "Be faithful to Him, and yours will be a glorious kingdom. Nevermore will Israel be slaves while you serve the LORD our God!"

Solomon kissed the hands of his father, promising to follow his wishes. He declared that he would severely punish those who had been unfaithful to his father, and that he would set about building a glorious temple to The LORD, as David himself had wished to do.

Meantime, Adonijah had not abandoned his hope of becoming king. Hatching a plan to deceive Solomon's mother, Adonijah came to Bathsheba, begging her to please him with one small request.

"Beloved mother of our worthy king!" began Adonijah. "I acted wrongly against your son, and against David, our father. Yet in his mercy, King Solomon spared my life. I ask for nothing now, other than you might grant me one small request!"

"Let your wish be known," responded Bathsheba, "And by my word, you will have whatever you ask."

"My request is this," continued Adonijah. "I would like to take Abishag the Shunammite as my wife. Please petition King Solomon to grant my heart's desire!"

Bathsheba did not realize that by marrying Abishag the Shunammite, who had been queen to King David, Adonijah would establish a new claim to become king. She then went to the king in ignorance, to petition him on Adonijah's behalf.

"Your brother Adonijah came to me, begging that I come before Your Majesty, to make one small request," began Bathsheba.

"Tell me, mother, what is this request," answered Solomon. "You know well that my heart desires to please you."

Bathsheba then related what Adonijah had asked for, believing that her son would take delight in her request. Yet Solomon did not respond kindly toward her.

"What an outrageous suggestion!" screamed Solomon. "What Adonijah is asking for is nothing less than my very kingdom. For this treachery, he must now surely be put to the sword!"

Solomon then gave orders to his men to find Adonijah, and strike him down. There would be no mercy shown toward him this second time. Adonijah was then slain, and all threats to Solomon's claim to be the rightful king of Israel came to an end.

Solomon was determined to keep the promise that he had made to his father David, to faithfully serve God. He sought to be a fair and noble king, but he doubted his own ability to make wise decisions. Being still young, he lacked experience in matters of state, and found it hard to judge between what was right and what was wrong.

Solomon then retreated to a place outside his city called Gibeon, which was known as a special place for making sacrifices to the Lord.

Solomon made many sacrifices of his own, coming before God with a yearning heart, and full of humility.

"What troubles you, My son?" asked God. "Tell Me what is on your heart."

"Mighty God," began Solomon. "I am troubled because I fear that I am not yet ready to serve You and Your people as king of a great nation.

"I am but a young man, and lack wisdom to know what is right and what is wrong. Please grant me the gift of discernment, that I may rule wisely, and so well serve both my God and my people."

God was very pleased to hear Solomon's request.

"You have not asked for great riches, nor glory for yourself," answered God. "For this reason, I grant not only that you be full of wisdom, but will give to you those things that you have not asked for too. Your kingdom will become very great, and your fame will spread throughout the world!"

Solomon prostrated himself once more before the altar, declaring his love for God, and expressing his gratitude for all that God had given him.

Solomon quickly became known for making wise judgments. He was consulted by high officials and lowly field workers alike. His decisions were made based on sound insight, and the rich meaning of his words struck home with all who heard them.

One day, two women came to Solomon's court to seek his judgment, each claiming that a baby that they brought with them was their own.

Barely hesitating before suggesting a means by which to determine who was the true mother, Solomon proposed that the child be sawn in half, so that each woman might have their share of the infant.

"This I cannot bear," protested one of the women. "Let my opponent have my child, so that its life is spared." Meantime, the other woman considered the king's proposal to be a suitable solution.

"Were my child to be cut in half, then I could never face the sun again," cried the woman who had made the protest.

Seeing that she was driven to save the life of her child, even if this meant that the other woman might take him, Solomon knew that she was the infant's true mother. He therefore judged in her favor, and she was reunited with the crying baby.

The king made many more wise decisions of this kind, sometimes inventing similarly clever means by which to determine the truth. He gave wise counsel, and wrote down many of his words of advice.

He wrote beautiful songs too, and gained deep knowledge in all manner of subjects in both the sciences and the arts. All who heard him speak were impressed with his wisdom. God never failed him when he needed to find an answer to a difficult question.

Such was the fame of Solomon's greatness, that many traveled from afar to visit him. Kings and queens from distant lands numbered among those who sought his advice. They brought rich gifts, and made treaties with him, promising not to go to war with this very gifted king, who they felt sure must be blessed by God.

One famous visitor who traveled many miles to test Solomon with her questions was the Queen of Sheba. This powerful queen traveled across Arabia with a long caravan of camels, bearing fine spices and precious jewels from her rich and enchanting land.

"They say that you are the wisest among men," said the queen, when she stood at last before Solomon's throne. "I have come to seek your wisdom regarding many things, and in return, bring you luxury gifts from my kingdom."

The king had no difficulty answering all the questions that the queen put to him. They debated together for many hours, and formed a strong friendship. The queen then returned to her own kingdom feeling enlightened, and pleased that she had made a friend in such a powerful ruler.

Many others also sought an audience with Solomon. The king formed an alliance with the pharaoh of Egypt, and acted kindly towards his neighbor in Tyre, and each of the governors in his own kingdom.

The king of Tyre gave Solomon countless quantities of cedar and juniper wood, as well as promising that the Israelites could take as much stone as they wished from his vast quarries.

In turn, Solomon sent wheat and olive oil to Tyre, so solidifying a friendship that had grown strong during the time of his father David.

Solomon used the stone that was quarried in Tyre, and the cedar and juniper wood that was floated down the river from there, to construct the most magnificent temple to God that has ever been seen.

The temple took seven years to build, needing the labor of many thousands of men. Its exterior gleamed with the dressed stone that Solomon had taken from Tyre, while its interior was made from the cedar and juniper wood that had also been brought from that neighboring kingdom.

Magnificent statues of angels and cherubim were installed inside the temple, while its innermost sanctuary was overlaid in gold. Here, finally, was a fitting place to honor The LORD, and a suitable place to become home for the Ark of the Covenant, which contained God's written commandments, and had been carried by the Israelites all the way from the deserts of Sinai.

Solomon also commissioned work to begin on a magnificent palace for himself, which he furnished with the many gifts that had been brought to him by visiting kings and queens. This too was fashioned in the most spectacular way. Its towering columns were made of fine marble, and its walls of polished cedar were lined with gold.

Solomon ordered that a new throne be made for himself. This too was the finest of its kind that had ever been seen. The throne had a giant circular back, encrusted with emeralds, onyx, and pearls. Its arms were made of gold, and its base of ivory.

The throne sat upon a plinth, which was reached by six finely-polished marble steps. Beside the king's seat sat two statues of lions, made from pure gold. Sculptures of other animals lined the steps too–eagles, wolves, peacocks, and more.

Throughout his kingdom, the king commissioned new works. Impressive buildings were erected, and statues were cast in marble and gold, proclaiming the king's wealth and majesty.

Yet God was troubled when he saw that Solomon had begun to stray from his promise to honor Him.

The king delighted in the riches that he had acquired through God's blessing, and he began to covet even more. He even began to allow some of his household to worship gods other than the God of Israel, turning a blind eye when they made sacrifices to these false idols.

God then spoke to Solomon, warning him that He was very displeased that His servant had forgotten his promise to always serve Him.

"All that you have I have given to you," said God, "Everything that you see, and all that you set your feet upon is yours solely because I have given it. I have melted the hearts of kings and queens from distant lands, and made them to be friendly towards you. It is I Who granted you wisdom, and I that inspired the songs that pour out from your mouth, and the writing that flows from your pen!

"Since you have disobeyed me, Israel cannot continue as a united kingdom. I will allow a division to occur in this land, but not before your reign is ended!"

God then set some of Solomon's supporters against him. Even one of his most trusted advisors conspired against the king, but his plot was revealed, and so he fled to safety in Egypt.

Despite his failings, Solomon ensured that the Ark of the Covenant was brought to the temple that he had built to honor God, and he dedicated what the people of Israel had long waited for–the creation of this magnificent place of worship to the God who had delivered His people from suffering.

Solomon reigned for forty years before he died. He was buried in the city of David, being laid to rest beside his father and other ancestors.

Never before had the world known a ruler as wise as he. Never since has there been any who has lived in such splendor.

CHAPTER ELEVEN

Elijah and The Evil King and Queen

LONG AGO, in the Kingdom of Israel, to the east of the great Mediterranean Sea, lived an evil man called Ahab, who came to be king in his land. Ahab married an equally evil woman named Jezebel. Together, they reigned in their kingdom for more than a full score years.

Unlike the great kings David and Solomon, who had reigned over all Israel before him, Ahab did many things that displeased God. In fact, he did not worship the God of Israel at all, but Baal, and he erected a giant column to honor the mother goddess, Asherah.

Ahab turned away from pleasing The LORD, and he did many terrible things.

At that time, God had sent a good man to warn his people and the evil king that they must turn their hearts back to the true God of Israel. This man was called Elijah, who is among the greatest of God's servants ever to have lived. He spoke the words that God breathed into him, just as do all His faithful prophets.

Seeing the evil that Ahab was doing, and being called by God, Elijah came to the king and warned him that because of his evil, no rain would fall in the land for years to come. Only if Elijah pleaded with God to end the drought would water fall from the sky once more.

Yet Ahab refused to listen to Elijah's warning. So Elijah traveled to a place that was to the east of the Jordan River, coming beside a small stream, where God told him he might take water.

"Never will you go thirsty, nor your stomach yearn in hunger!" promised God, "For you are My obedient servant, and I will always hold you close to My heart!"

God told Elijah that he would instruct ravens to bring him food every day. And so it was, that each morning and each evening, Elijah was brought food by a flock of these magnificent black birds.

No rain fell in the land, as God had forewarned, and in time, the stream from which Elijah took his refreshment itself ran dry.

"Now where will you have me go?" begged Elijah, prostrating himself in prayer before his Lord.

"You must now go to a place called Zarephath, which is in the land of Sidon," instructed God. "There you will meet an old and weak widow, who will fetch you water, and provide you with food."

Elijah then journeyed for many days to reach the distant place that God had told him to find. When he arrived, he saw an old woman making for the city gates, just as God had described. She carried with her a small sack filled with flour, and a jar bearing a little olive oil.

"My dear lady!" cried Elijah, "May it please you to offer this humble man a little of the food that you bear, and show me to where I might find water?"

"My good man, this I cannot do!" replied the woman, "For I have only a small quantity of flour, and no more than a tiny drop of olive oil. This I must take for myself and my son. I fear that this alone will not be enough to save us from starvation, and that soon we will surely die!"

Undeterred, and trusting God's Word, Elijah persuaded the woman to use the flour to make a small loaf of bread for himself, as well as to feed her own mouth, and that of her son.

Unsure about Elijah's intention, the woman nonetheless agreed to his plan. It was then revealed to Elijah that the woman would not lack for food nor drink while the drought continued.

And so, Elijah stayed with the woman and her son, while their needs for food and drink were satisfied by The LORD.

In time, the poor woman's son became very ill, and finally, he could breathe no more.

"What is this that you have done?" cried the woman to Elijah. "How can it be that you say that you are a man of God, while in your presence, my son has now departed us?"

Elijah was deeply saddened by the woman's grief. Firstly, her husband had departed her, and now she also mourned for her son.

"My God, why have you allowed this to happen to this poor woman?" pleaded Elijah. "I beg you to bring joy into this house once more!"

Elijah then carried the boy in his arms, taking him to an upper room of the house, where he laid him down on a couch.

There, Elijah stretched himself over the boy's body three times, crying out that God might restore his life to him.

God saw Elijah's pleading, and heeded his cry. And so God brought about a wonderful miracle–the boy's life was returned to him, and both the widow and Elijah sang songs of great joy and praise to The LORD!

After three full years since the drought began, God told Elijah to return across the desert to come face-to-face once more with the evil king, Ahab.

"I will restore life to the land again! " promised God. "I will send rain to fall upon the land, and crops will grow once more, and the people and animals will live!"

Elijah then set off on his way to confront the evil king.

Meantime, Ahab had called upon his trusted servant Obadiah, who was charged with looking after his palace's affairs.

"Soon there will be no food for our horses, donkeys, and mules!" lamented Ahab. "Let us then go out to see what grasses and other food we may find. I will lead my party in one direction, and you go forward in the other!"

Obadiah was obedient to his king, but he also honored the God of Israel. When Queen Jezebel set about killing all the prophets in the kingdom, Obadiah had taken one hundred of these loyal servants, and led them into two caves, where he ensured that they received food and water, and could live safely in secret.

Obadiah continued to pray to God, seeking ways to ensure that God's children would not fall victim to Ahab's evil schemes.

When he set off along the road as Ahab had commanded him, Obadiah saw a man approaching from the opposite direction. This he recognized to be Elijah.

"My Lord, how pleased I am to see you!" exclaimed Obadiah, when the two men came face-to-face.

"You know that I serve the true LORD, even though my duty is to oversee the affairs of the palace. So it is, that one hundred of your fellow prophets hide safely in my care."

"You are indeed a good man," replied Elijah. "Today, I beseech you to take me quickly to meet Ahab, for this is what The LORD has commanded me to do!"

"My dear friend," replied Obadiah, "This I cannot do. For if I tell my king that Elijah is here, and he cannot find you, I will surely be put to the sword! We have sought you in many lands, and required that their leaders swear that you are not hidden in their protection. So it is, that the king will deal very severely with me if I return to him, entreating him to offer you an audience with him, but then you disappear once more!"

Elijah recognized Obadiah's concern, but assured him that it was God's Will that he should meet with Ahab.

"Take me to your king!" demanded Elijah, "This is what God commands!"

Obadiah then did as Elijah requested, and Ahab came to meet him.

"Is this Elijah that I see before me?" hollered Ahab. "You, who have brought misery upon our people!"

"It is not I that has brought about misery," retorted Elijah, "But you and your people, for turning away from honoring God!

"Let it to be known whose is the true God! I challenge you to summon the many prophets of Baal and Asherah, and call upon all your people too, to meet me upon

Mount Carmel. There, you may build an altar to your gods and sacrifice a bull, but not set it alight. I too will do the same, calling upon my God to bring fire to eat up my sacrifice! May your many hundreds of prophets call upon your god to do the same! This way, we will know whose God is true, and whose is false!"

Ahab consulted with his advisors, and they agreed to face Elijah's challenge. The many prophets and people from across the land were summoned, and they gathered to meet Elijah at the top of the sacred mountain.

When dawn arrived, Ahab's prophets built an altar from wood, then laid the pieces of a bull upon it, which they had made ready after killing the magnificent creature.

They then called upon the name of Baal, and to Asherah too, crying out to the gods most beloved of Ahab and Jezebel to bring fire upon the altar and to consume the sacrifice that they had made ready.

All morning they called upon their gods, beating themselves and stomping their feet, crying out for an answer ever more desperately. But no fire came to take their offering.

By lunchtime, Elijah started to laugh out loud at their hopeless pleading.

"Well, your gods are taking their time!" he joked, "Perhaps today is a holiday for them, or they are taking their noonday rest?"

The people and the prophets ignored Elijah's taunting, not giving up their pleading. All day, even until the time of the evening sacrifice, they did not cease from offering their prayers. But still no fire came.

As dusk was falling, Elijah stepped forward to prepare his own altar. He took twelve large stones to build it with, representing the twelve tribes of Israel. Then he dug a large trench around the altar, and instructed that water be poured over the dead body of the bull that he had sacrificed, even overflowing into and filling the deep trench.

Turning to face the setting sun in the sky, and casting his eyes out over the many miles of land that stretched before the mountain, Elijah opened his arms out wide, and called out to his God.

"My God, make known Your power!" he pleaded. "Let it be seen that You are the true God, who never deserts Your people, nor allows them to fail!"

No sooner had Elijah uttered his prayer, than a terrible fireball fell upon the altar, immediately burning the bull's flesh and bones to cinders, and even drying out all of the water that filled the trenches!

When they saw what had happened, the people of Ahab were terrified.

"Surely this is the true God!" they cried. "How we have been deceived and led astray!"

Elijah then commanded that all of the prophets of Baal and Asherah be seized and put to death. He then told the people that God would send rain, and that they should hurry down from the mountain, even though no cloud could yet be seen in the sky.

When the people had gone, Elijah bent down on his knees, crying out again to God. "Let the rain now come," he pleaded. "Let the famine now end!"

While he did not see it at first, in time, a small cloud appeared over the distant sea. Elijah then rushed down from the mountain himself, overtaking those who had gone before him. Soon, the sky became very dark, and thunder roared. Rain beat heavily upon the land, flooding rivers, and bringing life to the fields once more.

Ahab came to his wife Jezebel, telling her all that had happened. Yet her heart was not turned toward God, and she vowed to put Elijah to the sword, just as he had fated for her beloved prophets.

When Elijah got wind of her evil plan, he feared for his life, and fled across the desert. After many days of wandering, he fell beside a bush, praying that God might take his life. Afraid and weary, he felt that he could no longer continue his journey.

Yet the time was not yet right for Elijah to return home to be with his Lord, and God sent an angel to comfort his servant.

"Look behind you! Here is some bread that has been freshly baked for you!" cried the angel, "And too, God has supplied water for you, to give you strength to continue your journey!"

Elijah ate the bread, and took the water, regaining his strength and trust that God continued to have a plan for him.

He then wandered in the wilderness for a full forty days and forty nights, before eventually coming to rest in a cave by the side of the Mountain of Horeb, which was sacred to God.

God then spoke to Elijah.

"What are you doing here, My son?" asked God.

"I am terrified, my LORD!" answered Elijah, "For I am alone among Your prophets now, and the evil king and queen of Israel covet my blood! These evil people have rejected You, and do not respect Your altar. Yet I know that You are the true God!"

"Do not be afraid!" replied God. "Go stand on the mountain, for I am about to pass by!"

Elijah then did as God had instructed, turning toward the mountain. The earth then trembled, and rocks fell from on high. The very spine of the mountain was ripped apart, and there followed a howling whirlwind and a terrifying earthquake. Yet Elijah did not see God appear amidst this terrifying spectacle.

Instead, he heard a gentle whisper calling to him once more. "What are you doing, My son?"

Elijah repeated his fear and anguish for the state of Ahab's kingdom, and God commanded him to return to the Desert of Damascus, where he was to anoint two new kings, and also to find and anoint a ploughman who would become his successor, whose name was Elisha.

Elijah then journeyed again across the desert, anointing the new kings as God had commanded. God told him that he would protect seven thousand of the Israelites who had not succumbed to worshipping Baal or Asherah.

When he came to Elisha, Elijah found the man who was destined to follow him working in the fields. There, Elisha was driving a yoke of oxen, ploughing the land.

Elijah threw his cloak around Elisha, and told him that God had chosen him to be his successor. And so Elisha set aside his work in the fields, and followed behind his new master.

In the Kingdom of Israel, Ahab heeded the warning of a servant of God, whose instruction enabled him to be victorious in battle against the king of a rival land.

Yet he was quick to turn away from God again, when the moment suited him.

One time, one of the prophets of Israel disguised himself with a headband and came before Ahab.

"My Lord!" called out the prophet, "During the battle, I was set upon and ordered to keep watch over a man who had been held captive. They told me that if he were to slip my guard, my own life would be in jeopardy. Yet this man is no longer by my side!"

Since he saw that it was his role to pronounce judgment on the man that now stood before him, Ahab then replied, "You declare your own punishment. So it is, that your life should be taken in place of the one that you have lost!"

The prophet then removed his headband, and the king recognized his true identity.

The prophet then spoke severely to Ahab, pronouncing what The LORD told him: "You have let go free a man that I destined should die!" the prophet said. "So will your life be taken!"

Angered by what he had heard, Ahab then stormed back to his palace.

Ahab was a jealous man, and he coveted many things that others had.

Close by his palace was a vineyard, which was owned by a man named Naboth. Ahab wanted to have this vineyard for himself, so he summoned Naboth to appear before him, making a proposal to buy the land from him, or to offer another vineyard in its place.

Naboth refused the king's offer, saying that he would never allow the land of his ancestors to be taken.

Ahab then returned to his chamber, where he sulked and cursed the man who had denied him his greedy wish.

When she saw what a state her husband was in, Queen Jezebel derided him, mocking him for not being a stronger ruler, being able to stand up to those who taunted him.

"I will get that vineyard for you!" declared Jezebel. "No one will call me weak, nor hold on to what is rightfully mine!"

Jezebel then set about a plan to entrap Naboth, and bring about the seizure of his land. She drafted letters in the name of the king, taking his own seal to them. These she sent to the elders of Naboth's city, instructing them to declare a day of fasting, but to offer Naboth a distinguished place among the people.

"Find two scoundrels to follow close by Naboth," she wrote. "When there are many witnesses who might hear their claims," she continued, "Tell these scoundrels to bear witness against Naboth, declaring him to be an enemy of the king, and one who utters false words against God!"

Believing the letters to be by royal command, the elders did as Jezebel described. They called a day of fasting, and appointed Naboth a distinguished man among their number.

They then found two scoundrels, and instructed them what they should do. When the time seemed right, these men came forward, offering their false witness against Naboth.

Condemning him for his supposed treachery, Naboth was then taken out from the city, where he was stoned to death.

When the elders reported back that Naboth was dead, Jezebel was delighted. She then commanded that his vineyard be taken into the property of the King.

God then told Elijah to come to Ahab, bringing warning of God's anger for what had happened.

"You have taken the land from a man that has been murdered in your name," Elijah angrily announced. "So it is too that your life will be taken from you while you writhe in pain, and your blood will become the drink of dogs!"

Ahab was troubled by what Elijah told him, and humbled himself before God. So God destined that his death would not be so cruel. But He did not assure the same for Queen Jezebel.

There had been peace in the Kingdom of Israel for some time, but soon Ahab sought counsel about whether he should go to war against the rival king Aram, seeking Aram's land known as the Heights of Gilead, which Ahab claimed as his own territory.

Forming an alliance with Jehoshaphat, king of the Kingdom of Judah, whose son was married to Ahab's daughter, the two men prepared to go into battle.

"Let me go in disguise," proposed Ahab, "But you put on your royal robes."

Ahab and Jehoshaphat then mustered their forces, and set off to face the army of Aram.

King Aram had instructed his troops to only lay hands on Ahab. All others were not to be taken.

When they saw Jehoshaphat in his royal robes, Aram's men made as to capture him. Jehoshaphat then cried out, whereupon they recognized that it was not Ahab that they saw before them. Yet an arrow had been shot at random, and this buried itself between a space in Ahab's armour, dealing him a mortal blow.

The evil king then died, and his blood spilled out upon the chariot that he had ridden into battle. His men took their king away to be buried, and washed the chariot at a pool in the land of Samaria. There, dogs licked off the blood stains from the chariot's wheels, just as Elijah had prophesied.

Following Ahab's death, Elijah continued to give prophecy, as God commanded him.

On one occasion, he met with a captain and a party of fifty men, who had been sent by the new king of Israel to meet him.

"Come down from your hill if you are a man of God!" cried out the captain.

"God will pour fire down upon you if I am truly a man of God!" replied Elijah. And so it was, that God sent fire from heaven, which consumed the captain and all of his party!

The king then sent another captain with a company of fifty men to meet Elijah. They again challenged Elijah to come down from the hill, but Elijah repeated what he had told the previous captain, and his group of fifty. These too were then consumed by fire.

A third time, the king sent a captain. Yet this captain bowed down before Elijah, professing that he trusted that he was truly a man of God. So Elijah went down from the hill and traveled with the captain to meet the king.

"You have turned away from God!" proclaimed Elijah. "For your wickedness, you will surely die!"

And so it was that that the king gave up his last breath, just as Elijah had prophesied.

Elijah knew that his days of wandering would soon be over. Elisha and the other prophets too knew that they would soon be separated from their master. Elisha then asked that Elijah would impart his spirit to him, and Elijah promised that he would never leave him.

While they were walking together, they came upon the River Jordan. There, Elijah took off his cloak, rolled it into a ball, and struck the water with it!

In an instant, the fast-flowing waters of the river separated, making a path for Elijah and Elisha to safely tread to cross to the other side.

They continued their journey, but at some point were separated when a chariot and horses that appeared to be engulfed by fire came upon them. Elijah was taken into the chariot and brought up to heaven in a whirlwind and amazing display of light that stunned all who witnessed it.

Elisha was in awe of what he saw, but knew that the charge that had been given to Elijah was now his responsibility to bear. And so he took Elijah's cloak, which had fallen from him, and struck the water of the River Jordan, as his master had done before him. So the river divided, as it had for Elijah, and Elisha crossed safely to continue prophesying the Word of The Lord.

As for Queen Jezebel, her fate was to be just as Elijah had foretold.

When he became established as Elijah's successor, Elisha instructed one of his followers to anoint Jehu, who commanded the army of Joram, the new king of Israel. Blessed with God's guidance and support, and following His command, Jehu sat about destroying Joram and all the descendants of Ahab.

Finally, he came to the city of Jezreel, where Jezebel was living.

When she heard that Jehu was approaching, Jezebel put on her finest clothes and make up, and waited by the window of her upstairs chamber to greet the commander as he passed by.

"You have killed your king, but do you now come in peace?" she called out, when Jehu arrived before her.

Looking up to the window where Jezebel stood, Jehu cried out, "Are there any among you who will follow me?"

Tending to Jezebel were two manservants, who heard Jehu's cry. They trusted that he was following God's purpose, and so they seized their mistress and hurled her from the window!

Jezebel's blood spilled onto the walls and drained into the dirt of the street below.

Jehu then went into the house, where he rested for awhile. He commanded that his men carry Jezebel's body to a place where it may be buried. When they came outside, the men saw that nothing but her skull, feet and hands remained.

Trampled underfoot by horses, and her blood licked up by dogs, Jezebel died a terrible death, just as had been promised would be her fate.

Together with her husband Ahab, Jezebel had lived her life of evil for more than twenty years. Yet when she died, no peace was assured for her body, and no future was destined for her offspring.

If we live like Ahab and Jezebel, we may enjoy the thrill of our wickedness for awhile. But in God's time, our false happiness will soon be ended, and we will give up God's love and grace.

Let us then not be like the evil king and queen, but like Elijah and his servant Elisha–always faithful to the one true God!

CHAPTER TWELVE
Esther, The Brave

THIS IS THE STORY OF a humble woman named Esther, who came to be queen over all of Persia, and through her bravery, helped save her people from certain death.

Our story starts before Esther came to be queen to King Xerxes, the man whose heart was stolen by her.

Xerxes was a very powerful ruler–his kingdom stretched from the deserts of Egypt to the mountain-tops of India. Elders, and nobles, and powerful military men from many regions were under his command, and the magnificence of his palaces was famous throughout the land.

The king wanted to show off his great riches, and to let the people of the city of Susa, where he resided, marvel at the splendor of his home and many possessions. So when he had been king for three years, Xerxes called a celebration, culminating with a sumptuous banquet, which lasted a full seven days!

All who came to the palace, including many nobles and people of high rank, saw the magnificent marble, onyx, and mother-of-pearl with which the king's home was ornately decorated. Soft velvet rugs covered the couches, and dancing fountains played in the courtyards, their water tumbling and glistening in the bright sunlight, like the ever-flickering reflections that shine from an elaborate crystal chandelier.

No food was spared for anyone who came to the banquet, and wine flowed freely–being served in goblets made from pure gold!

The king was delighted with everything he saw, but he wished to introduce his wife to his friends, so that they might admire her beauty. Xerxes' wife, whose name was Queen Vashti, had also arranged a banquet for the wives of the noblemen, elders and military commanders who had been invited to the king's feast.

When the king's servant came to Queen Vashti, making known his request that she present herself to him, the queen refused. Instead, she continued her own party, and told the servant to tell the king that she would appear at a time of her choosing.

When the king was brought this news, he was furious. He tugged at his hair, and banged his fist on the wide marble arm of his magnificent throne.

"How dare this woman disobey me!" hollered the king. "I reign in my kingdom, and no one must refuse my command–not even my wife!"

The king was beside himself, and called his advisors, to seek their counsel on what he should do.

"Beloved Majesty!" the advisors began, "No one must make a fool of you! This evil woman must be punished. No more must she be your wife. And because of her disobedience, no more may any wife in your land refuse the wishes of her husband!"

The king was pleased with what his advisors told him, and immediately issued a decree to put their advice into effect.

Those were very different times from our own, when many men thought that they were more important than their wives.

After a time, King Xerxes was persuaded that he might find a new wife, for it was thought fitting for him to be attended to by a beautiful queen. So it was, that many unmarried women were brought before him, to see if any might be his companion. But none seemed suitable to become his wife.

There was living in the city of Susa at that time a man named Mordecai, whose family had been brought there in exile from their home land in Israel. Mordecai was a Jewish man from the family of Benjamin, and he had taken into his care his niece Esther, who had been left an orphan at a young age. Mordecai loved Esther, and looked after her as though she were his own daughter.

Now Esther was very beautiful, and it came to pass that she was to be presented to the king as a possible suitor for him. When he saw Esther, the king's heart was filled with love for her, and he longed to make her his wife.

Esther lived in a special room in the palace for many months before she was formally introduced to the king. There, she was treated kindly, and given every help to prepare herself for the moment when she would come before the mighty Xerxes, ruler over all of Persia!

Her uncle had warned Esther not to make known that she was a Jew, for he feared that to declare this might not be in her favor. Esther did as her uncle advised, and did not make known her people's heritage.

One day, while he was resting by the city gates, Mordecai overheard a conversation between two men, who were plotting to kill the king.

When he heard their devious plan, Mordecai went to his niece, beseeching her to warn the king about what he had heard. Esther followed Mordecai's advice, and gave credit to her uncle for reporting the intended treachery.

When the incident was investigated, Mordecai's testimony was found to be true. So it was, that the two men who had plotted against the king were seized, and their bodies were hanged from the tallest scaffold.

Of all the king's advisors, a man named Haman was his most esteemed. The king decided to appoint Haman his second-in-command, giving him authority over all other elders and noblemen. The people of the land were expected to bow down and honor this much favored statesman, much like they would do for the king himself.

Yet Mordecai refused to bow down before Haman. Day after day he refused to honor the mighty man of court, attracting the attention of two of the celebrated man's advisors. When they told Haman about Mordecai's refusal to honor him, and made known that he was a Jew besides, Haman was furious.

Rather than choose to punish Mordecai, Haman hatched a plan to bring terror among all the Jews of the kingdom. In an audience with the king, Haman pretended that none of the Jewish people honored the king, and argued that should they be allowed to continue their supposed disobedience, they might soon bring about trouble within the kingdom.

"Your Majesty!" began Haman, "Allow me to suggest that you deal with this people once and for all, so that they may no longer be a threat to you!

"If it pleases you, allow me to oversee their destruction. In return, I will pay you ten thousand bags full of silver!"

"Do as you wish, my trusted servant!" commanded the king. "I do not need your money, and give you my authority to strike down this people, and take hold of their property!"

Haman then set about his evil campaign to kill the Jewish people and seize their property, bringing terror across the land.

When he saw what was happening, Mordecai tore his clothes and put on sackcloth. He wandered around the city, crying out loud, as he grieved for his beloved people. In cities and villages across the vast kingdom, there was much wailing and mourning, as the king's orders were put into practice.

Mordecai sent a message to his niece, begging her that she might present herself to the king, where she might petition him to end the tyranny.

Yet in the reply that she gave to her messenger to bring to Mordecai, Esther feared for her own life.

"My dear uncle," she explained, "For me to present myself before the king is not as easy as you may imagine. He has not called to see me now for more than thirty days. You know that for any person to approach the king when they have not received his summons or the touch of his gold scepter is an offence that's punishable by death! Not even I, his queen, may be spared this terrible fate!"

Mordecai was not persuaded by his niece's reply, and again sent her a message, imploring her to reconsider the fate of both herself and that of all of her people.

"My beloved child!" Mordecai pleaded, "It is true that you must be very brave to face the king without his invitation, but I fear that if you do not, your very life will be in danger, just as it is for all of our people! I beg you to meet His Majesty, and to plead our case!"

With great trepidation, Esther eventually came round to her uncle's point of view. Firstly, she begged her uncle that he might persuade the fellow Jewish people who were known to him to fast on her behalf for three full days, and to pray to God for her safety.

"When the fasting is over," she declared in her message, "I will then present myself to the king. If he chooses to take my life, then so it will be. I know that I must not let my people down!"

Mordecai then sent word for the Jews of the city to fast, as Esther had requested. When the three days of fasting was over, Esther summoned all her courage, and presented herself to the king.

Rather than being angered by her presumptuous appearance, Xerxes was delighted to see his queen, for he was consumed with love for her. Without hesitating, he offered her the touch of his golden scepter, making known that she was welcome in his presence.

"My beloved queen!" the king began, "What favor do you ask of me? Be assured, that whatever you wish, I will provide for you! Even if you desire half my kingdom, this will be yours!"

"If it pleases Your Majesty," Esther began, "The greatest desire of my heart is that you and the noble Lord Haman might join me tonight for a banquet that I have prepared for you!"

Esther's proposal delighted the king, and he gave order that the queen's invitation be made known to Haman, such that he might also join them for the feast.

When they ate with Queen Esther that night, the king again asked his wife what request she might make of him.

"My dear Lord," replied Esther, "What will please me most is if your Glorious Majesty and Your Excellency, Lord Haman, might join me again in my quarters tomorrow evening, such that we may share a feast such as this once more!"

The two men then returned to their quarters, delighted with Esther's proposal.

When he came to his house, Haman called together his friends and other noblemen to make known the special treatment that had been afforded to him.

"You can see my many riches, and know that I am held in the highest esteem among the king's advisors!" Haman bragged. "I know that I am worthy of such honor, but it gives me no pleasure to see that disobedient Jew Mordecai loitering outside the city gates. That man refuses to bow down to me, not paying respect to one such as I, who is deserving of great praise! Yet tomorrow, I will go again with the king to meet with Queen Esther–I alone am permitted to dine in their majesties' company. What an important man am I!"

Haman's friends and his wife were impressed by his bragging. To boost his sense of self-importance even further, they suggested that he should not delay in putting an end to Mordecai.

"Have a giant pole put up outside your house," they suggested. "Hang the one you say does not obey you on top of this pole, such that all will see what happens to those who do not honor you, as you deserve!"

Haman was delighted with this suggestion, and set about having a pole erected. Meantime, he readied himself for his second visit to the queen's quarters.

Before evening came, which was the time that Queen Esther had proposed for her husband and Haman to meet her in her quarters, Haman went to the courtyard of the palace, planning to seek an audience with the king, where he might obtain his consent to have Mordecai hauled up onto the pole.

The king was in his throne room, looking back on the many events that had come to pass during his reign. His attendants read from the annals of this time, which recorded the many things that had happened in the kingdom.

Among the events that were brought to the king's memory was the action of Mordecai, in saving the king's life, by revealing the treacherous plan that had been hatched by the two men outside the city gates.

"Was any honor ever shown to this man who acted so loyally toward me?" asked the king.

"No, Your Majesty!" replied his advisors. "This man now wanders like a beggar outside the city gates, and has even taken to wearing sackcloth!"

"Bring Haman to me!" then commanded the king, "For I want to seek his counsel on how to honor such a man as this."

Haman then came before the king, expecting to have an opportunity to seek his permission for Mordecai to be taken away and put to death.

"What might be a suitable honor for someone who shows total loyalty toward their king?" asked Xerxes.

Thinking that the king was talking about himself, Haman thought for a moment about how he would most want to be honored, then gave his reply.

"For such a person as this," he proposed, "Only the highest honor can suffice! I propose, Your Majesty, that one of your own robes be made available for this person to wear, and a fine horse from your own stables brought out for him to ride!

"Let him parade around the whole city, where the people may sing praises to him, and declare him their hero. Such is what is deserved of a true servant of the king!"

"What a splendid plan!" chuckled the king. "Let this be done right away! I appoint you, my closest advisor, to ensure that this comes to be!"

"Who then is it that is deserving of this high honor?" Haman then eagerly asked, certain that it was he that the king wished to show favor to.

"Why, it is Mordecai, the Jew!" replied the king. "For it was he that saved my life!"

Haman could barely disguise his shock and anger at hearing the king's command, but he feigned a smile, and retreated to his home. Knowing that he must obey the king's will, Haman then arranged for Mordecai to be dressed in a royal robe and be led through the city streets on a horse that had been chosen from the king's own stables.

That evening, Haman joined the king and Queen Esther for their planned banquet.

"Tell me once more, my dear lady," asked the king, "What request you will make of me?"

"Ask me anything, and it will be yours–even if you desire to have half of my kingdom!"

"My dear Lord," replied Esther. "The greatest desire of my heart is that the great misery that has fallen upon my own people, your Jewish servants, be ended. Many have already been killed, and their property has been taken. Were we to become your slaves, I would not make such a request of you, but soon I fear that all of my people will be gone from your kingdom forever. Yet we have done you no wrong!"

"Who has brought about this destruction?" commanded the king. "Who is responsible for this great terror?"

"That very man is before us now," answered the queen, bowing her head, and trembling in fear for her life. "It is by Haman's command that so many have been put to the sword!"

Enraged by what he heard, the king rushed from the banqueting room into the courtyard of the palace. He stomped his feet, and ran around the courtyard in a fury.

Knowing that he had brought the king's anger upon himself, Haman rushed to the couch where the queen was reclining. He stretched himself over her, meaning to beg her to plead for his mercy when the king returned.

At that moment, the king came back into Esther's room. Seeing Haman lying besides his wife, Xerxes believed that his evil advisor was making to attack her!

"See that even now, this scheming traitor wants to take my wife from me!" hollered the king. "How shall I punish one such as he?"

"There is a large pole that has been set up outside Haman's house," observed one of the king's servants, who had now joined him. "Perhaps if it meets with His Majesty's approval, this might be where one who has acted so wickedly be hanged!"

So it was, that Haman was taken away from the palace, and hauled upon the very pole that he had erected earlier, expecting this to be where Mordecai would meet his end.

Meantime, Mordecai was dressed in the finest robe, and made a companion of honor to the king. The king gave orders that the terror against the Jews should stop, and indeed, that any act against them be punished by death, and the property of their aggressors be taken.

The king commanded that Haman's estate be taken from him, and that all his sons be killed. He decreed that his wealth be given to Esther, who became even more precious in the king's sight.

Following the king's command, Jews across the land gathered in their homes to celebrate their freedom from tyranny. They put any who challenged them to the sword, just as the king commanded, killing first five hundred men in the city of Susa, and then three hundred more in that very city, as well as seventy-five thousand people across the entire land. Yet they did not take ownership of the property of those they killed.

Even today, Jewish people remember this time of celebration, and give gifts to each other and to the poor in memory of what Mordecai and Queen Esther, with God's help, brought about for them.

Queen Esther lived handsomely, issuing edicts with the king's authority.

Her faithful uncle Mordecai also lived a life of abundance. Now it was he, rather than the evil Haman, who was elevated to be the king's closest and most trusted advisor.

Bravely he fought for what was right, and bravely his beloved niece represented her people before the king. Because of their faithfulness, God ensured that they would have a magnificent destiny. So our story ends happily, just as it may for any who are faithful to God.

CHAPTER THIRTEEN

Job, A Troubled Man

MANY YEARS AGO, in the land of Uz, far to the east of the Mediterranean Sea, there lived a man named Job.

Job was a faithful man, always following what God told him to do, thanking Him for all that he had. Even when his sons and daughters celebrated each year's harvest with a healthy feast, Job always prayed to God for their forgiveness, in case any of his children had acted wrongly.

God blessed Job with many gifts. He owned thousands of sheep, hundreds of oxen, and so many camels, that if they were lined up one behind another, their line would stretch toward the far horizon! The produce of his land was bountiful, and Job was highly regarded and given honor among his countrymen.

It was said that Job had never done any wrong. Every day, he begged God for forgiveness for anything that he had said or done that might have offended his LORD.

God was very pleased with his loyal servant, and showered him with many favors.

One day, the devil came to God, bragging about all the mischief that he had been creating, as he went to and fro' across the earth.

"See how I have caused many people to turn away from You!" laughed the devil. "The people only worship You when they need Your help. But they are quick to set their hearts on all that I offer when their lives are not in danger!"

"Have you considered My loyal and beloved servant, Job?" countered God. "He is blameless, and never ceases to trust in Me, and sing My praises!"

"Well, of course he is happy to," argued the devil, "For You give him everything that he needs. You have blessed him with many livestock, and given him a happy family that supports him. Were you to take these things away, then we might see whether this faithful servant will continue to be so loyal."

"So be it," said God. "I will allow you to do your evil work with my servant, but you must spare his life. Persecute him, and take away the things that I have given, then we will see what My beloved son makes of his test!"

The devil then went away from God, to set about his evil plan.

Sometime later, as Job was resting in his house, a servant came running up to him.

"Master! Master! I bring you terrible news!" cried the servant. "I was working in the fields with other servants. Suddenly, a fearsome raiding party set upon us, stealing your oxen and donkeys. We had been ploughing the fields, but were helpless to stop them, as they were many in number, and came brandishing clubs and swords. They killed all of your servants, except for me. I managed to hide at a distance, then came quickly to tell you all that happened!"

Even while the servant was speaking, another of Job's laborers came running up to his house.

"Master! Master! A great tragedy has fallen upon you!" hollered the servant, almost struggling for breath, since she had run many miles to bring her master the urgent news.

"While your children were gathered at your son's house," she continued, "A fireball descended from heaven, then it tore through the house, killing all who were within it. Only I survived, as I was gathering water for your son's party when the terrible fire storm appeared."

No sooner had this second messenger related her story, than a third from among Job's servants came running towards him.

"Master! Master! I bring news that I wish were not true!" shrieked the servant. "While I and others of your servants were working in the fields, thieves set upon us, taking all of your sheep, and putting your other servants to the sword. Only I was able to escape their rampage."

When he heard all that happened, Job could hardly control his emotion. He tore at his clothes, and hurled himself onto the ground, clasping his head in his hands, and letting out a loud scream.

"What person can bear such news as this?" bewailed Job. "Who before has been beset with such a tragedy, even within a single day?

"I am but a man, and I do not understand why I should suffer this way. Yet I know that I was born naked, and when I die, so shall I return naked to my God."

Job's wailing continued throughout the whole day, and well into the night. Yet this unwavering servant of God did not accuse his LORD of acting wrongly.

After all these terrible things happened, the devil again came to speak with God. God asked the devil where he had been.

"I have been traveling far and wide, causing mischief throughout all the world!" the devil chuckled. "I have succeeded in turning many of your servants to follow me! Soon, there will be no one who will worship Your name!"

"Have you not witnessed the faith of my servant, Job?" challenged God. "Even though he has faced many tragedies, he has not held Me to blame, nor sworn his allegiance to any but I!"

"This may be so," the devil remarked, "Yet I have not inflicted pain on Your servant's body. Anyone who suffers physical distress will surely quickly desert You!"

"So be it!" replied God. "I will allow my precious son to suffer terrible pain, but you must not take his life from him. Then we will see how my servant is tested!"

The devil then departed from God's presence, and went about causing further mischief throughout the world.

God allowed his servant Job to be afflicted with a terrible condition. Blisters and sores covered Job's skin, from the tips of his toes to the very top of his head.

Job rested outside his house, where he knelt down on the dusty ground, beating his hands against the earth, and sobbing a torrent of tears.

"How wretched am I!" screamed Job. "What person can bear such affliction? What will be my fate? These sores and blisters I can hardly bear, and my heart is full of anguish."

Job's wife tried to console her husband, but he could not be persuaded by her words.

"Why will you not curse God for all that has happened?" demanded Job's wife. "Then He will take your life from you, and your problems will be no more!"

Yet Job refused to put blame on God for his suffering.

Three of Job's friends heard about his suffering, and came together to the place where he was resting, hoping that they might be able to offer him words of advice and comfort.

These men, whose names were Eliphaz, Bildad, and Zophar, were horrified when they saw the state that their dear friend was in. Such was his distress and so unsightly was his physical appearance, that they too tore at their clothes, and wondered what words of theirs might possibly comfort such a man.

For seven whole days and seven whole nights, Job's friends sat with him without speaking a word. Nothing came to them that they believed could help offer hope to their friend.

Eventually, Job opened his mouth to speak.

"Perish the day that I was born!" he cried. "May all memory of that day be erased forever, since it would have been better had I never left my mother's womb! Were I gone from the earth now, I would be at peace. No more would I suffer, nor face the tragedies that have beset me!

"What person should face the fate that has been dealt to me? Once, I had all that I needed–my sons and daughters surrounded me, and I was celebrated among my countrymen. Many came to me seeking advice, or requesting favors. I honored their requests, as any diligent person should do.

"My fields stretched for many miles. Thousands of livestock were under my care, and my servants toiled from dawn to dusk, keeping me well provided for, and serving my every need.

"Throughout all my days, I served God with a pure heart. To Him alone I swore my allegiance, never departing from doing what is right.

"Now, my days of happiness are ended. I bury my face in the sand, for the sun no longer shines kindly upon me. I am the most wretched among men, and it would be better had I never been born!"

Job's friends were very saddened to hear him speak this way. Never before had they seen their friend in so much distress, feeling helpless and in dread of his situation.

One by one, each of the three friends came forward to offer their advice. Eliphaz was the first to speak.

"Beloved friend," Eliphaz began, "How it grieves us to see you so troubled. You have spoken about your love for God, and about this, there can be no doubt. Yet, you claim that you have never done wrong. Surely, no person is without fault? Can there be anyone who has never acted nor thought wrongly against God, even if their failing remains hidden from them?

"Confess the errors that you may not see, dear friend," urged Eliphaz, "For you have surely done wrong in God's eyes, even though you believe that you are innocent."

Eliphaz could not console Job.

"I cannot remain silent, nor deny that my suffering justifies anything less. Let my complaint be heard, for there is no wickedness on my lips!" asserted Job.

"Where are you now, my God, to hear my cries?" bewailed Job. "If I have done wrong against You, make known Your servant's failing. Punish me, or forgive me for my iniquity. Yet, You do not appear to relieve me of my guilt."

Bildad then came forward, to see if he could offer any words that might encourage Job to confess the failings that he might not see.

"Dear friend," Bildad began, "You are a worthy man, but surely are not without any blame? Why would God allow suffering for one who has never committed wrong against Him? Surely there is none born of human flesh who has not once strayed from serving God?

"Your children may have been punished by God for misdemeanors that you do not see," continued Bildad. "Our lives are over in a brief moment, yet we assume that we are very important! Look at the stars in the sky. How many can you count?

"See the world around you, which has survived longer than we can ever imagine. The Moon reflects the light of the Sun. Yet, for all we know, perhaps even this is imperfect in God's sight.

"How can you claim to be without any fault?" challenged Bildad. "You are only a man, and are but a speck of sand in a desert of unfathomable vastness when compared with the greatness of God. Confess your wrongdoings, my dear Job, and God will surely hear your prayer!"

Job then answered his friend.

"I am blameless, yet I am powerless to defend my innocence before God. What mortal human can hold court with one that is as mighty as He? What grain of sand can contest the vastness of the desert?

"God created the heavens," Job agreed. "He causes even mountains to move, and allows the earth to tremble under our feet. He does as He wills, and can treat the evil and the innocent as one. I know that I have done no wrong against Him, yet I am helpless to defend my case before Him. My days are numbered, and it would be better for me were my end to come quickly!"

Job continued his complaining, beating his fists against the ground, and shedding many tears. His friends remained silent for a long time, as they witnessed his distress. Another younger man stayed with them too, who listened carefully to what each of the three friends had to say.

Zophar then stepped forward to offer his counsel. Unlike his two friends before him, Zophar believed that Job was not listening, and that he needed to be told very firmly that he should not continue to deny that he was without blame.

"Beloved Job," began Zophar, "We know that you are a man worthy of much honor, yet you deceive yourself when you claim that you are blameless before God!"

"How can it be that you believe that your wisdom is as great as the wisdom of our LORD?" Zophar demanded. "Do you believe that you have power to search inside the depths of every soul, or to discern what God sees in His perfect understanding of our secrets and desires?

"What makes you believe that you are an equal with God?" Zophar continued. "What arrogance pretends that any human being can know what God knows, or see what God sees? Confess your failings, for you are not an equal to God. Plead with The Almighty for forgiveness, for then God will save you from your affliction!"

Job listened carefully to his friend, but could not be persuaded that his complaint was unfair.

"God does not answer me now!" moaned Job. "I know that what you say about Him is true. No one compares with God. None has His wisdom; none may make lives easy or hard as He wills. Yet my complaint is justified! I wish for an audience with God. If only there were one who could mediate between us, such that my case could be heard. I am sure that my argument is flawless. I have acted faithfully. But alone, I cannot prove my innocence."

Job's friends continued to encourage him to see good reason. Job argued his case further for a long time, continuing to plead his innocence. Broken in spirit, Job saw no end to his suffering. Nor did he believe that God would come to his rescue.

After a long time, the man who had observed the three friends' appeals to Job, whose name was Elihu, ventured to offer his own advice.

"I am but a young man," started Elihu. "I have listened to the counsel of your three friends. While I lack their experience in years, I beg that you might allow me to say what is on my heart.

"Your friends are right to declare that no one compares with God," Elihu observed. "His designs are beyond comparison. None can compare with His power. His wisdom no person can fathom. The workings of His Universe are magnificent to behold!

"See how He sends the snow in winter to bring moisture to the dry land. Witness the passing of the seasons, and their part in making ready, giving life to, and yielding their abundant riches–supplying nectar for the bees to make honey, fallen leaves from which the birds of the trees can build their nests, and a bountiful harvest to feed our own mouths.

"He sends the rain to allow the crops to grow, and provides shelter for the most humble of His creatures. Who can deny the majesty of His work, nor claim to understand the mystery of His Creation?

"In His divine wisdom and glory, God brings blessing for everyone. None are denied a witness to the miracle of His provision. We can be sure that God does not take pleasure in seeing the suffering of those who are faithful to Him!"

Once Elihu had spoken, a furious storm descended upon the land. Dust and sand gathered in the wind, churning and spitting out in all directions. Then, from the midst of the turmoil, God spoke directly to Job.

"I am The Almighty, The One God who created you, and all of Creation, everyone that has gone before you!" boomed God. "I bring the snow, the rain, the winds, and the storms to clear the ground. I allow the sun's light to beam down upon you, lighting your days, and warming your body. At night, the stars that you see were all created by Me. Can you unbuckle the belt of Orion, or cause the Great Bear to stray from its decreed place in the sky?

"What human can know what I alone know? Do you count yourself an equal, or one who can fathom the infinite mysteries of the Universe, whose secrets I alone have knowledge of?

"Do you know when the time is right for the mountain goat to give birth to its young? Do you know where the eagle flies when it is time for it to return to My home? What creatures swim in the dark oceans that you know of, and which might you be able to hook and tame, as though you were training a dog?

"Speak to me, if you can! Tell me what you know. Prove to me your might, if it is equal to Mine. What is it that you know that convinces you that your wisdom is greater than Mine?"

When God had spoken, Job finally saw the error of his ways. He knew that his complaint against God was unjustified, and that God had never forsaken him, nor denied him His blessing.

"Almighty God," cried Job, "You have tested your servant, and I have been found to doubt You. Who can deny that none is greater than You? No one understands the mysteries of Your ways, nor can fathom why You allow suffering. Yet I know that this was for my own good, for my soul now yearns for Your love even more than before. Please forgive your doubting servant, for I now see that I am not beyond blame!"

God was very pleased that Job still desired to follow Him, and was satisfied that His faithful servant no longer doubted that He always has a purpose in allowing everything to happen.

God then chastised Eliphaz, Bildad, and Zophar for doubting their friend, and commanded them to apologize to Job, and seek his forgiveness.

Job then lived happily for many more years. God blessed him as He had before. Job's brothers and sisters celebrated with him, and in very little time, Job became the owner of more livestock than he ever had before, and once again, became respected among the people of his land.

Few people are tested the way that God allowed Job to be tested. Yet we now know that God always has a purpose in everything that is allowed to happen in our lives. It is for us to stay faithful, even if at times, it may appear that God has not heard our prayer. We can be sure that He is always listening, and that He always ensures whatever is best for us.

CHAPTER FOURTEEN
Daniel, The Dreamer

IN ANCIENT TIMES, there lived a powerful man named Nebuchadnezzar, who was feared throughout the world. His vast kingdom stretched from the Mediterranean Sea far into Asia. Its capital city was the largest that the world had ever known. No expense was spared in furnishing Nebuchadnezzar's palaces. Rich, velvet drapes hung from the walls, and imposing marble columns reached up to the tall ceilings. Lively fountains played in the open courtyards, while gleaming, golden and multi-jeweled ornaments decorated the rooms in which the king held his court.

A disagreement arose between Nebuchadnezzar and a rival king, Jehoiakim, who reigned in the neighboring land of Judah. With his mighty army, Nebuchadnezzar quickly defeated the Judeans. He then seized their treasures, bringing them back to his own palace in the city of Babylon.

The tyrant king decreed that some of King Jehoiakim's family and noble followers be brought into his own service. These included young men of noble birth, of fine appearance and strong physique, who looked as though they might become capable servants. Among these was a young man called Daniel, and three compatriots, Hananiah, Mishael, and Azariah.

Those taken into Nebuchadnezzar's service were required to undergo training for no less than three years. They were given new names, taught the Babylonian language, and expected to adopt their captor's customs, some of which were offensive to them. Food that was forbidden by the Judean religion was served at their table. However, Daniel was so appalled at the prospect of eating such food, that he appealed very strongly to the official who was in charge of the captives' education and housing.

"My Lord, I cannot eat the food that you give us!" pleaded Daniel, "For it is offensive to my religion!"

"Insolence!" barked the official. "You have been given this food freely, and have been spared your lives by our generous king. Do not dare to refuse our hospitality!"

Still, Daniel refused to eat the food, continuing to make his protest.

In time, the official's heart was melted by God, causing him to have pity upon Daniel.

When he next saw Daniel, he asked him what might happen were he to agree to Daniel's request.

"I am not without a heart," the official began. "But my duty to the king is clearly stated.

"If you continue to refuse our food, then the king will see that you do not grow strong and healthy like those of your countrymen who do accept our hospitality. Then, it will be my head that meets the executioner's sword, for I know what happens to those who are unfaithful to our king!"

"My Lord, I promise you that this will not happen!" replied Daniel. "Allow your servant to make a proposal. Set aside ten days for your servant, and several of my companions, to be tested. Let us eat only vegetables and food that is acceptable to us during this time, while you continue to serve others from among our number the food that is presented at the royal table. If, at the end of this period, those who have refused the diet of your people appear weaker and less capable than those who have been served the food that you prescribe, then I will concede that your concern is justified!"

The official pondered this plan, and considered it reasonable to allow it to be put to the test.

For the next ten days, Daniel, and three of his trusted companions, Hananiah, Mishael, and Azariah, were served only vegetables and food that was suitable for them, while others who had been brought from Judah were fed food that was considered palatable to the Babylonians.

When the experiment was completed, to his astonishment, the official observed that Daniel and his friends were healthier than those who had eaten the food offered at the king's table. In fact, their cheeks were rosy, their skin was pure, and they appeared to be strong, and full of energy.

"How can this be?" the official enquired. Still, he was now convinced that his life would not be in danger were he to permit Daniel his request. And so, from that moment forward, Daniel and his companions were served food that was not offensive to their religion.

Three years after they had been taken into his service, Daniel and his fellow Judeans were brought before the king, such that he could choose from among them who would serve him personally.

The king was very impressed with Daniel, Hananiah, Mishael, and Azariah. They appeared to be in the rudest health, could speak fluently in the Babylonian tongue, and offered the king many words of wisdom. Nebuchadnezzar knew of no others who demonstrated such capability, and so he was moved to appoint them among his personal servants.

God blessed Daniel and his friends with many gifts, including powers of diplomacy, and wisdom to understand riddles and mysteries. To Daniel, He gave the ability to interpret dreams. The young men became well known for their abilities, and were counted among the wise that gave counsel to the king.

It happened that the king had a terrifying dream. In vivid detail, he was shown a giant statue, crowned with a head of gold, and with its body and arms made of bronze, silver, and iron. Its feet were partly made of bronze, and partly of clay.

In his dream, the king then saw a huge rock striking the statue, shattering it into many tiny pieces. These pieces were carried away by a harrowing wind, while the rock that had destroyed the statue grew into a giant mountain, growing and growing until it consumed the whole Earth.

The king was deeply troubled by the dream, and yearned to know its meaning. He then sent for the magicians, sorcerers, astrologers, and sage men that advised him.

"I must hear from you the detail of my dream, and know what it means!" demanded the king.

"Tell me what you see and what it means. If you can do this, I will clothe you in the finest jewelry and richest silks, and make you great among men. But if you fail, I will tear down your houses, and cut your heads from your bodies!"

"Mighty Majesty, tell us your dream, and then we will interpret it for you!" implored the magicians, sorcerers, astrologers, and sage men.

"Are you trying to make a fool of me?" retorted the king. "First tell me what I dreamt, then I will know that you're not trying to deceive me!"

Seeing that the king had presented them with an impossible demand, the magicians, sorcerers, astrologers, and sage men were deeply troubled. Their protest had made the king very angry, and it seemed that no one could persuade the feared Nebuchadnezzar that any person alive could know what had been dreamed by another.

Eventually, the king had enough of hearing their protests. He summoned his guards, commanding them to bind the wrists of the magicians, sorcerers, astrologers, and sage men, and take them away to await their execution.

He also commanded that all the magicians, sorcerers, astrologers, and sage men in the kingdom be found, and that they should face the same fate as the men that he believed had made a fool of him by their pretended wisdom.

When the king's guards came to Daniel, meaning to seize him and his companions, Daniel spoke very tactfully to the chief guard, in order to learn what had brought about the king's wrath.

When the guard explained what had transpired, Daniel pleaded with him to petition the king to give him an audience.

"With God's help, I may be shown this dream," offered Daniel. "If it is the Will of The Almighty, then not only the content, but the meaning of the king's dream will be made known to me!"

Reluctantly, the chief guard presented Daniel's petition to the king. Doubting that Daniel could delay his own execution, and the deaths of those who were awaiting the same fate, Nebuchadnezzar nonetheless agreed to allow Daniel a little time to see if he could reveal the dream to him.

Daniel cried out aloud to God, beseeching Him to give him wisdom, such that he, and his friends who had also remained loyal to God, might be saved.

God looked kindly upon Daniel, and revealed to him the very dream that had so troubled the king. God also told Daniel what the purpose of the dream was, such that he could explain its meaning to Nebuchadnezzar.

"My Dear LORD," cried Daniel, "My Creator and Beloved–how I honor You for Your mercy! All praise to You for Your provision! My words alone can never express my gratitude to You, The One Who always spares His people!"

Daniel then came before the king, where he prostrated himself, and kissed the feet of his human master.

"Mighty Majesty, ruler over the greatest kingdom on Earth, allow me to describe your dream!" Daniel confidently declared.

"In your dream, you saw a magnificent statue. It had dazzling beauty, and towered high above the ground. Its head was made of gold, and silver encased its hands and arms. It had a stomach and thighs formed from bronze. Its legs were fashioned from iron, while its feet rested firmly in their casting of bronze and clay. No sight that has ever been seen was as awe-inspiring as that of the statue that you saw in your dream!

"While you were gazing at the statue in wonder," continued Daniel, "A giant rock flew toward it, striking its centre, and causing it to crumble into thousands of tiny pieces. Even the golden head was shattered, and the fine metal dust that fell to the ground was quickly carried away by a powerful wind. The rock that brought about the statue's destruction formed into a towering mountain, growing in size to fill even the entire Earth!"

The king listened in amazement as Daniel described the dream exactly as he had received it. Yet he remained silent, hoping that Daniel might now be able to reveal the meaning of what he had seen.

"Your Majesty, let me now explain what this strange dream means!" continued Daniel.

"You, mighty king, have been given dominion over the greatest kingdom that has ever seen. When you reign no more, another kingdom will replace yours, yet it will not be as great as yours. You are the head of gold, but arms of silver are worthy of a lesser king. A third kingdom will later rise up to replace the second, one that you see in the statue as the belly of bronze. Finally, a kingdom with the toughness of iron will come to be, which will overcome all the others.

"Yet this will be a divided kingdom, as the statue's feet are made of both iron and clay. While it will be strong, it will also be brittle. As clay is prone to fracture, so there will be disharmony among its people.

"God Himself will then install His own Kingdom, which is far greater than any kingdom known to man. This kingdom will crush all others, and it will endure forever. This is the rock that destroyed the statue, and the mountain that towers higher than the eye can see! This, Your Majesty, is what the true God has revealed to me, and I know that the words that I speak are guided by Him!"

For a time, the king was unable to reply. Such was the power of Daniel's oratory, and so accurate the detail of his description of the dream that the king had witnessed, that the king fell to his knees, prostrating himself in front of his own servant!

"My closest sages could not offer me this explanation," the king eventually opened up, "Yet you have revealed every detail of my dream. Surely, yours is the true God! From this moment, I appoint you as one of my closest advisors. Many riches will be bestowed upon you, and I grant you the right to choose other ministers for me as you will!"

Daniel thanked the king, and recommended that three of his trusted companions join him in high offices of state–Hananiah, Mishael, and Azariah.

It was not long before Nebuchadnezzar turned away from praising the God of Daniel to honoring one of his own choosing. He even decreed that a giant idol be made from gold, and be erected on a fertile plain, not far from his palace.

When it was installed, this imposing impression of a false god was nearly one hundred feet high. People traveled from far around to wonder at this remarkable creation.

The king then ordered that prefects and governors from all over the kingdom should attend a ceremony to dedicate the idol. When all were assembled, the king's herald shouted aloud the royal command: "Let it be known when the sound of the horn, and the lyre, and the harp, and pipe be heard, that every person must fall to the ground and sing praises to the golden idol! Anyone who disobeys this command will be immediately thrown into a furnace, which will burn with flames that are so hot that the bodies of those who are taken there will immediately be burned to cinders!"

When the people heard the decree that the herald had delivered, they were terrified. Yet none present were ready to defy the will of the king, and risk being thrown into the furnace.

There were only a few who refused to follow the king's orders. These were the loyal servants of God–

Daniel, and his three companions, Hananiah, Mishael, and Azariah.

There were at that time astrologers who despised the Judeans, who had become so well esteemed in the king's sight. Seeking to cause them harm, they came to the king, appealing to him to punish those who would not bow down before the golden idol.

"Your Majesty!" the astrologers' delegation began, "You have rightly ordained that all people must bow down before the golden idol whenever beautiful music is played. Yet there are those among your subjects who insist on disobeying your command. We beseech you to punish those who are disloyal to your Majesty, who disrespect the golden image, just as you have ordained!"

The king then sent for those that the astrologers accused of disobeying his order–Hananiah, Mishael, and Azariah.

"Is it true that when the horn, and the lyre, and the harp, and pipe are sounded, you refuse to bow down and worship the golden idol?" questioned the king. "Are you so insolent that you refuse to obey my command?"

Hananiah, Mishael, and Azariah bowed before the king, yet they were untroubled by his probing.

"This is indeed true, Your Majesty," the three replied. "Ours is the true God, and the only one that we worship. So it will be, that if you will bind us and have us thrown into the fire, our God will rescue us. But even if He does not appear, we will not bow down before the monstrous idol that you have created!"

Hearing the three companions' brave response sent the king into a furious rage. He ordered that the strongest men from his army bind the three defectors, then throw them into a furnace that had been stoked to be seven times hotter than normal. Such was the heat of the furnace, that the soldiers themselves were incinerated, even as they threw the three men into the burning cauldron.

Yet, Hananiah, Mishael, and Azariah did not perish. God sent an angel to rescue them, protecting them from the violent flames that tore around them.

Astonished, Nebuchadnezzar saw the three men walking around within the flames, together with the angel who guarded them. Approaching the furnace, the king shouted out to them, imploring them to come out from the furnace, now that his eyes had been opened to see Who was the true God.

So it was, that Hananiah, Mishael, and Azariah came out of the furnace, and they were completely unharmed. Not even a single hair on their heads was singed, not a mark could be seen on their bodies.

"Yours is the true God!" declared Nebuchadnezzar. "You were faithful even until death, defying my orders, but opening my eyes to the lies that have been sold to me! For your faith, I will make you great among men. Now, for those who do not praise the true God that has been revealed to me, a special punishment is reserved! Their bodies will be cut into many pieces, and they will endure the fire of the hottest furnace!"

King Nebuchadnezzar believed that the God of Hananiah, Mishael, and Azariah was the true God, but he found it hard to stay faithful to Him. Such was the king's power and greed, that Nebuchadnezzar craved for more worldly things, to increase his wealth and standing in the eyes of his subjects and rival kings.

As he had before, God then spoke to the king in a dream. As before, its meaning was obscure.

In this new dream, the king saw a huge tree, whose canopy stretched as high as the sky, and spread out to the left and right, far and wide. Birds of many kinds nested in its branches. Other animals made their homes in its sturdy boughs and hiding places, while below, animals of the land rested safely under its protection.

The tree's leaves were strong in texture, finely colored, and healthy; its abundant fruit amply fed all the creatures that it supported.

In the dream, the king saw a messenger from heaven appear, commanding that the tree be cut down, leaving only a shallow stump, which was to be bound by bronze and iron.

"Let him be soaked in the dew of heaven, and become as a wild animal, living as they do, and eating only grass," declared the messenger. "Let this life of hardship continue until seven years have passed!"

The king was deeply troubled by his dream, as he had been before. He summoned his magicians, sorcerers, astrologers, and sage men, insisting that they interpret the meaning of what he had seen. But none were able to do so.

Finally, he commanded that Daniel be brought before him. He then repeated the dream, such that Daniel might explain its meaning.

As he had before, Daniel begged the king for a little time to pray, in order that he might discern what God would have him reveal.

Each day that passed, the king could see that Daniel was deeply distressed, and seemingly reluctant to make known what had been revealed to him. King Nebuchadnezzar then reassured Daniel that he was ready to hear whatever Daniel had to say, and so Daniel began his interpretation.

"Your Majesty, how I wish that this dream were intended for one other than you!" Daniel began.

"The tree that you saw represents yourself. You are a mighty king, having dominion over many people, and a richly blessed, vast land. You provide food and livelihoods for your people, just as the tree provides shelter and fruit for the many creatures that live within its protection.

"Yet everything that you have has been given to you by God. It is He that is the provider, yet you fail to honor

Him! What you have will then be taken away from you, just as the tree is felled. A stump remains, bound in bronze and iron, which represents the faded glory of your kingdom. However, if you come back to God–as you will once seven years have passed–both you and your kingdom may be restored to their former glory! Give thanks to God, turn away from oppressing the poor, and confess the greed and self-righteousness that is in your heart!"

The king was very disturbed after hearing Daniel's explanation. Yet he did not doubt that God spoke through this remarkable young man.

Just as Daniel had forewarned, the king's power soon faced a challenge. One night when the king was walking on the roof of his palace, a messenger from The LORD came to him and told him that he would be driven away by his people into the wilderness, where he would be soaked by the dew of God, and would eat grass like an ox.

This is what came to be. Just as had been shown in the dream, Nebuchadnezzar was humbled to live like an animal. His fingernails grew long, like the claws of an eagle, and his beard continued to grow until it touched the ground on which he walked. Hair covered his whole body, just like a bird's body is covered with many feathers. He ate grass like an ox, and wandered around aimlessly, always in search of shelter.

When seven years had passed since he was driven away from his palace, King Nebuchadnezzar finally recognized his failings, and called out to God to save him.

"Mighty God, now I recognize that You are the true God! Everything that I once had was given by You. I am wretched and have wandered far from you, one who has been destroyed by his own greed. I beg your forgiveness. I was so quick to forget you!"

God heard the king's prayer, and ordained that the people be accepting of him once more. Nebuchadnezzar returned to his palace, and his power was restored, just as his kingdom rose once again to become famous throughout the world.

Nebuchadnezzar praised God, recognizing Him as the true provider of everything that was given to him.

Sometime later, Nebuchadnezzar passed away. Belshazzar inherited his crown. Belshazzar reveled in his power, just as his ancestor Nebuchadnezzar had done before him. The new king cared little for his people, but only for himself. Instead of worshipping the true God, he made his prayers to idols made of stone, iron, bronze, and wood. He arranged wild parties in the palace, and did whatever pleased him.

One day, at a party that the king had called for his noblemen and women friends, Belshazzar ordered that the golden goblets and plates that had been seized by his ancestor from the temple of the Judeans be brought to him, such that they might be used by guests at the banquet. Wine flowed freely, and the revelers feasted themselves on the richest meats and choicest fruits.

Suddenly, in the midst of the partying, a hand appeared from nowhere, which then began inscribing some words on a plaster wall of the palace. The following is what was written:

MENE, MENE, TEKEL, PARSIN

The king and his guests were terrified by what they saw, unable to stop their knees knocking together. Not understanding the words, they puzzled over what the writing might mean.

Quickly, Belshazzar summoned his chief advisors, astrologers, and sages, begging them to tell him what the words meant.

"If you can explain the meaning of the writing," Belshazzar promised, "I will clothe you in rich robes, and endow you with great power."

The advisors, astrologers, and sages puzzled over the words, but just like the king and his guests, they were unable to discern their meaning.

The queen then came into the room. Seeing the king's distress, and realizing that nobody present could help him understand the meaning of the words, she told him about Daniel, and his special gift for interpreting dreams.

"My beloved husband," the queen gently whispered. "There is a man in your kingdom who gave counsel to your father when others were unable to explain the meaning of his strange dreams. This man will surely help you discover the meaning of the words that you see on the wall before you now!"

Daniel was then sent for, and the king repeated his promise to clothe him in the finest robes and elevate him to a position of great power if he might explain the meaning of the writing.

"This I will do!" promised Daniel, "However, I have no need for your riches. Give these to another."

Daniel then proceeded to explain the meaning of the words, but began with a stern warning for the king.

"Your father Nebuchadnezzar strayed far from God," reminded Daniel. "He worshipped idols, and thought himself worthy of great praise. Yet God humbled him, making him live among animals, even eating grass like an ox. For seven years he lived in the wild in a hopeless state, until at last, he acknowledged that all that had been given to him was the gift of God.

"You know this story well, yet you have not humbled yourself before The LORD! You even profane His glory by deigning to drink from the goblets and eat from the plates that were taken from His temple. You consider yourself to be deserving to have all that you have been given, and you make your supplications to idols made of stone, iron, bronze, and wood.

"Here, then, is what the writing that you see before you means: your days are numbered, and your reign will soon come to an end. You have been weighed and found to be wanting. Your kingdom will be divided and shared between the Medes and the Persians."

Satisfied that Daniel had given him a true explanation, Belshazzar ordered for Daniel to be clothed in fine robes and made a high minister in his court. Even that very evening, the king was slain, bringing his reign to a speedy end, just as the writing had prophesied.

A new king then came to the throne, whose name was Darius. Darius was impressed with Daniel, who often gave him wise counsel and served him diligently in his court. The king therefore planned to make Daniel overseer over all other ministers and advisors in his kingdom.

When they got wind of this, a group of advisors over whom the king wanted Daniel to have charge began to hatch a plan to discredit their new master.

They debated among themselves, but could not decide any obvious means by which they could bring charges against Daniel.

"He's too clever by far," they concluded, "And he does no wrong. We'll never find a way to make a case against this rascal!"

Eventually, they decided that the only way that they could trap Daniel would be to encourage the king to enforce a law that would make it illegal for anyone to pray to God, as Daniel did diligently every day. They then sought an audience with the king to present their proposal.

"Glorious Majesty!" they began. "Should it please Your Majesty, we propose that a month of celebration be declared in your honor. Let no one worship anyone or any god during this time, other than giving thanks to you, celebrating your excellent person!"

The king then signed into law a decree that prevented anyone from worshipping or praying to any god for a period of thirty days.

Delighted that the king had accepted their proposal so easily, the men then went to wait outside Daniel's house. After a short while, they saw him kneeling close by a window, speaking his prayers to God aloud.

The men then entered Daniel's house, and seized him, binding his wrists, and leading him through the streets to face the king.

The men then sought an audience with Darius, which they were quickly granted.

"Your Majesty, have you not signed into law that no one should pray to God during the thirty days of your celebration?" asked the men.

"This is indeed true," replied the king.

"Is it not also true that any who defy this law be punished by being thrown into a den of hungry lions?" continued the men.

"This I have also decreed," confirmed the king. "Any person who defies my will deserves to face the most terrible punishment."

"Then your majesty must know that your servant Daniel has disobeyed you!" announced the men. "We caught him praying in his room this very day, and there are others besides who can testify to this!"

The king was deeply troubled when he heard this news, for he wanted to find a way to save Daniel from the fate that awaited him. Even by evening time, the king could not find a solution to his dilemma. Therefore, very reluctantly, he gave orders that Daniel be taken and placed in a pit that was also home to a pride of hungry lions. A lid was placed over the pit, and the king's seal impressed upon it, in order to assert that justice had been done, and that no one should dare attempt to rescue Daniel.

The king tossed and turned in his bed all that night, distraught that the life of his trusted servant Daniel had been taken because of his own decree.

At the first light of morning, the king rushed to the pit and cried out, hoping that the God of Daniel might have saved him.

"Daniel, my servant, are you still alive?" cried the king.

"I am still here!" replied Daniel. "I am not harmed! An angel of the LORD came to me, filling my heart with hope. He closed the mouths of the lions. Not one of those creatures rested its paws upon my body!"

The king was overjoyed to hear that Daniel had survived the night, and immediately ordered that he be released from the den.

Darius praised Daniel's God, knowing that it was He who had saved His faithful servant. The king made a new law, requiring that all people in the kingdom should now worship the true God.

The men who had attempted to entrap Daniel were themselves arrested, along with their families. The king decreed that their punishment should be the same as that that they had sought for Daniel. They were then taken to the den, and thrown into the pit where the lions were waiting. Yet their god did not come to rescue them. No sooner had their bodies landed on the floor of the den, than the lions pounced upon them, tearing at their flesh with their claws, devouring them in seconds!

Daniel lived happily during the reign of King Darius, and also his successor, King Cyrus.

Both before and during their reigns, he had other dreams, which were interpreted for him by an angel of God. Even what will happen at the end of times was revealed to Daniel.

The angel told him he would rest in God's protection until it was time for him to leave this life. Then he would be richly rewarded in heaven, as are all servants of God who never give up believing that He alone is the one true God!

CHAPTER FIFTEEN
Jonah, The Hesitant

IT HAPPENS SOMETIMES in our lives that we do not want to do things, nor go to places, which we do not like. Oftentimes, it is for our own good that we don't hide away from such things, and especially when we know that God wants us to do something.

This is, indeed, what a man named Jonah did many years ago, and his story that we now tell has become famous throughout all the world.

Jonah lived in Israel, and had been anointed by God to proclaim His message to His people.

One day, God spoke to Jonah, instructing him to go to the city of Nineveh in the foreign land of Assyria, and to tell the people there that they must turn away from their wicked ways, putting their trust and love in God.

"Jonah, My son, I desire that you take My Word to this wicked people," said God. "Tell them that if they do not relent from their wicked ways, that I will very soon bring total destruction upon their city. No animal nor person will survive!"

When he heard what God had told him to do, Jonah was very afraid. He felt certain that no one alive could convince the wicked people of Nineveh that they should turn their hearts to the God of Israel, and that he, a humble Hebrew, would surely be laughed at, and quickly turned away from the city.

What is more, Nineveh was a mighty city–perhaps then the largest that had ever been known. Its ruler was hostile to Israel, and its army was a formidable force.

Jonah therefore resolved to run away from the awesome commission that God had given him.

He seized a few of his belongings, and made quickly for the bustling port of Jaffa, where he hoped that he might find a ship that would take him far away from his homeland.

"If I journey across the sea," reasoned Jonah, "Then God cannot expect me to return to Nineveh!"

Jonah wandered around the harbor side, watching cargo of all sorts being taken onto and off of the lively boats that bobbed around in the blue water. He heard voices speaking in many different tongues, was enchanted by the colorful goods that the busily chattering merchants bore, and enlivened by the sweet smell of magnificent spices that were being passed between the ships and the jetties.

Soon, he came across a ship that appeared to be making ready to leave. He cried out to the captain, pleading with him to take him on board, in order that he could escape across the sea.

"Please allow me to journey with you!" begged Jonah. "I must leave this land quickly, for I'm afraid that my God wishes me to travel to a land where I do not wish to go!"

Seeing that Jonah might offer a useful pair of hands on board the ship, the captain agreed to allow him to join his crew. The ship was bound for the city of Tarshish, far away across the Mediterranean Sea.

Jonah quickly made himself useful on board, and related his story to the other mariners.

Once the ship left port, the captain ordered that its sails be raised to their highest point. The ship then started to make fine progress toward its destination. At first, the sea was calm. However, dark clouds soon appeared on the horizon, and a howling wind began to batter the waves, causing them to rock the boat from side to side.

In very little time, the ship was engulfed by a violent storm. Fierce winds battered its side, at times, threatening to turn it completely upside down. The captain ordered that the sails be lowered, and some cargo was thrown overboard, in order to lighten the load. Yet still this was not enough to ease the ferocious rocking of the boat.

Giant waves crashed over the deck, while torrential rain fell from the sky.

Never before had the captain and his crew witnessed such a storm. Fearing that the boat might capsize, and they would be drowned, each man on board started to pray to their own gods.

"Save us! Save us!" they cried. "Mighty gods of ours, calm the troubled sea, and save our trembling souls!"

One man who was not among those remaining on deck was Jonah. He had gone into a cabin at the very bottom of the boat, thinking that this was the safest place to be. When the captain found him there, Jonah was fast asleep!

"Wake up, you lazy scoundrel!" hollered the captain. "Get up quickly, and help us!

"How can you sleep through such a tempest?" shrieked the captain. "Join us now, and pray to your God. Perhaps He will be able to save us, for our gods are not answering our prayers!"

Jonah then prayed, as the captain commanded him, but the battering of the howling wind and the tossing of the boat amidst the towering waves did not abate.

The crew then decided to draw lots, to see which among them might be the cause of God's wrath.

It was Jonah who drew the shortest stick, and so the men questioned him about his motive.

"It is because I have disobeyed my God that this storm has come to be!" confessed Jonah. "I have run away from my God, and hidden from the purpose that He intends for me. For my disobedience, I must sacrifice my life.

"Take me, and throw me into the deep waters," Jonah continued. "Then the wrath of God may no longer be upon you. Perhaps in His mercy, He will calm the waters, and bring you to safety."

The crew listened carefully to Jonah's confession, and each man was greatly touched by his willingness to sacrifice his own life in order that they might be saved. However, they did not wish to be the ones who would send an innocent man to his death.

"You have spoken bravely," said one of the mariners. "Yet we must try even harder to plot our way back to land. Perhaps now that you have spoken your confession, God will show His mercy!"

The men continued to try to steer the ship toward land, but the power of the wind and irresistible strength of the waves made light of their efforts. Reluctantly, they eventually conceded that Jonah's plan was the only one that might save them.

So, with great pity for their fellow traveler, and crying aloud to God to not judge them for their actions, they seized Jonah, and threw him into the cold, dark water of the violent sea.

Immediately, the sea became calm, and the crew continued their journey to Tarshish.

The men were amazed at the sudden turnaround in their fortunes, but realized that it was by God's power that they had been saved. They then declared their praises to Him, and made offerings in gratitude for His great mercy.

Jonah, meantime, fell further and further into the depths of the sea. Yet rather than drowning and coming to a watery grave, God brought about a miracle that only He is able to–a giant fish, far larger than any person, swam towards Jonah, holding its gigantic mouth wide open. Before he knew what had happened, this magnificent creature had swallowed Jonah whole!

Jonah came to rest in the dry belly of the fish, which was not unlike being inside a huge cave. There he stayed for three whole days and three whole nights.

Jonah's journey into the deep before the fish swallowed him was a terrifying one. As he had fallen deeper and deeper, the water had become darker and more foreboding. Terrifying creatures came into sight, and he became wrapped in knotted, smelly seaweed. Lower and lower he went, until the pale sunlight that shone above the sea's surface could be seen no more.

When he finally came to rest inside the cavernous stomach of the fish, Jonah bowed down, and cried out in shame and terror to his God.

"Mighty God," Jonah began. "How I have disobeyed You! What a wretched person I am, and so foolish to believe that I could run away from You! You follow me everywhere, because You are everywhere!

"Almighty LORD, despite my disobedience, You rescued me! Even when I was tumbling deep into the dark waters, falling and falling, You had a plan to save me! Forgive Your wicked servant, and never more will I disobey You. If it is still Your Will, Mighty LORD, allow me to travel to the city of Nineveh, where I promise this time that I will not disobey You!"

God took mercy upon his servant, and caused the fish to rise to the surface of the sea and travel toward the coastline of Jonah's homeland, where it vomited out its human cargo.

Jonah landed face down in the sand, where he rested for awhile. He then pushed his hands against the muddy beach, slowly rising himself up to bring himself to standing, and then set about the long journey toward the celebrated city of Nineveh.

When he arrived there, the city was so large that it took three whole days for Jonah to walk around its streets. Everywhere he went, he cried aloud, "Turn away from your wickedness! Make peace with God. For if you do not, within forty days, you, and all your livestock, and every building and wall will be destroyed!"

Jonah did not rest from delivering the message that God had given him. He kept walking through every part of the city, and soon, all of its inhabitants had heard his words.

Such was the force of Jonah's warning, that the people were convinced that he spoke the truth. They prayed to God, and asked forgiveness for their wicked ways. Grieving for what they had done, they pleaded with God to allow them one further chance to be faithful to Him!

Even the king of Nineveh joined them. He took off his royal robes, and clothed himself in sackcloth, humbling himself before God. He then issued a decree to all of his subjects.

"Let everyone in the city turn away from wickedness!" the king commanded. "Let all take to wearing sackcloth, and pray that we might all be saved. Perhaps even now, if we are truly sorry for what we have done, God may still have mercy upon us!"

The people did as the king commanded, and God heard their prayers. Seeing that so many had been ready to turn their hearts back to loving Him, God had pity for them, and did not bring about the destruction that He had planned.

When he had finished his mission, Jonah went out from the city and came to a place in the desert where he might rest. There, he waited to see what might happen following the destruction that he believed God would bring about.

When he saw that God had forgiven the people for coming back to Him, Jonah was very angry.

"This is not fair!" complained Jonah. "Even when I was setting course for Tarshish, I knew that You are a gracious God, One Who is slow to anger. So it is that You did not punish this people, although they acted very wickedly toward You. It is better now that You take my life from me, for my anger is very great!"

God then spoke to Jonah in a gentle voice.

"Is it right that you are angry?" asked God.

Jonah continued to brood, but did not answer God. Soon, he fell into a deep sleep. God cared for the comfort and protection of His servant, so He caused a large plant to grow beside where Jonah rested, such that its leaves might provide shelter for him.

Yet when the morning came, God caused a worm to eat the leaves of the plant, exposing Jonah to the scorching rays of the sun. As the heat grew stronger, Jonah could bear his suffering no more, and he became faint.

"That wretched plant!" hissed Jonah. "Now that it has no leaves to protect me, I must face the sun's torture! It would be better for me to die!"

Hearing Jonah, God then gently spoke to him once more.

"Is it fair that you should be angry with this plant?" asked God.

"It is!" insisted Jonah. "I despise this plant, and wish that I would die!"

"My son," answered God. "I caused this plant to grow tall and healthy in a single night. Then it withered and died, even as the worm tore at its leaves. Yet did you once tend and care for the plant that offered you shelter? So too, there are many tens of thousands of people living in Nineveh, and many animals besides. Why do you suppose that I have no concern for them?"

God spoke gently, yet we do not know what Jonah then believed. His story ends with this question–did he come again to see that what God says is true, and humble himself once more, being faithful in God's service?

Perhaps it was that Jonah came to see that his anger toward God was not justified. God had rescued him from the most terrible plight and spoken gently to him, even when he felt alone and dejected. Perhaps he once again came to see that God desires the best for all His Creation, and that His plans are far beyond what any of us may imagine. Let us hope that this is the way that Jonah's story ends, and may it be our prayer for ourselves besides.

ACKNOWLEDGEMENTS

I would like to thank Sadelle Wiltshire for her kind assistance with proofreading and editing my original manuscript. Thanks are due too to Universitaria, for her stunning cover illustration.

Eternal thanks are due to The Great Creator, who inspires all ideas, and bestows the precious gifts of writing and storytelling.

The tales that are included in this book draw on more than one biblical interpretation of the story.

While biblical texts provide the basis for the stories, a storyteller's license is used to bring color and vibrancy to the text, while endeavoring not to detract from the messages and meaning of Scripture.

I have tried to open myself to be led by The Almighty in retelling the story, and trust and give all acknowledgement to God for what has been written.

All stories in this book are available as individual Audible audiobooks, and as separate titles.

Coming soon:

Tales Anew: Stories from The New Testament

Also available:

Fairy Stories & Fairy Stories (each story is also available individually, and as Audible audiobooks)
Arabian Nights & Arabian Nights

ABOUT THE AUTHOR

Clive Johnson is an interfaith minister, storyteller and retreat host. He has had a lifelong interest in the power of myth and the oral tradition of storytelling. He has no fixed home, pursuing a nomadic lifestyle that allows him to follow his heart. This is his eleventh book.

Clive may be reached via his website, www.clivejohnson.info.

www.ingramcontent.com/pod-product-compliance
Lightning Source LLC
Chambersburg PA
CBHW071727080526
44588CB00013B/1932